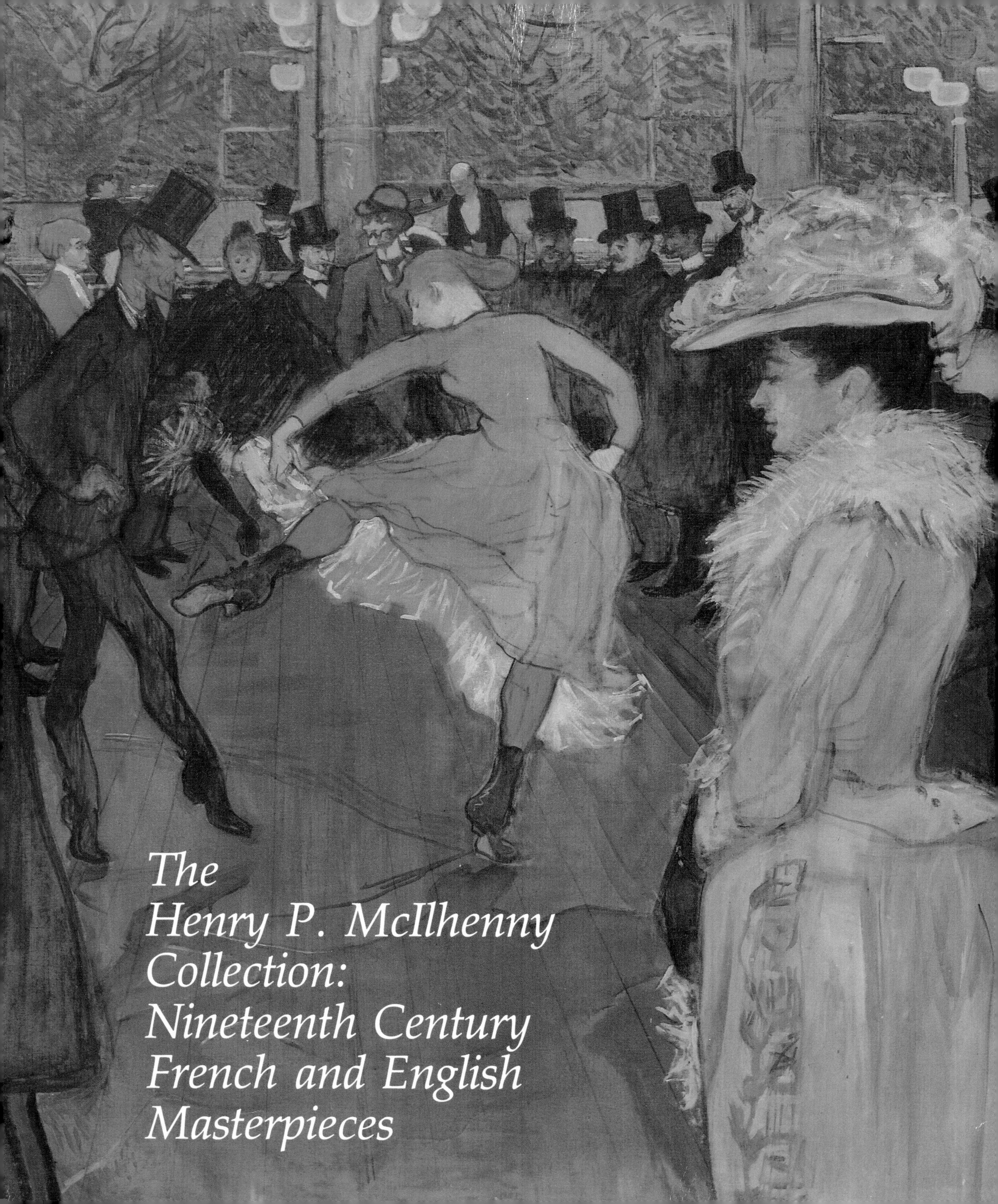

The Henry P. McIlhenny Collection: Nineteenth Century French and English Masterpieces

The
Henry P. McIlhenny
Collection:
Nineteenth Century
French and English
Masterpieces

The Henry P. McIlhenny Collection has been
brought to Atlanta by National Bank of Georgia.

The Henry P. McIlhenny Collection: Nineteenth Century French and English Masterpieces

May 25 - September 30, 1984

High Museum of Art
Atlanta, Georgia

Published by the High Museum of Art
Atlanta, Georgia

Editing by Kelly Morris
Design by Jim Zambounis, Atlanta
Transparencies by Will Brown, Philadelphia
Separations by W. Frank Gibson, Marietta
Printing by Preston Rose Company, Atlanta

Library of Congress Catalogue No. 84-80751
ISBN 0-939802-21-X

Cover: Henri de Toulouse-Lautrec,
At the Moulin Rouge: The Dance (no. 35, detail)

Foreword

The psychology of collecting art has been the subject of novels, art historical writing and museum chronicles. Its motivations and the implied romance of wealth and intrigue fascinate writers, and the idiosyncracies and shifting fates of collectors can become central to matters of taste as well as provenance.

We know that there are many motivations that drive individuals to collect objects, from intellectual curiosity to an obsessive need to possess things. Of all the reasons for collecting art, surely the instinct for aesthetic enjoyment is the best and ultimately the most rewarding, and it is this impulse which characterizes Henry McIlhenny's accumulation of great pictures. There is a sympathetic delectation, often tempered by a certain pathos, in such paintings as the neo-classical portraits, the incisive drawings by Degas or Landseer's remarkable dying ptarmigan. Mr. McIlhenny surrounds himself with these works in his home; he doesn't keep them in storage. Obviously the daily contact with these masterful examples of artistic insight is central to his spiritual wellbeing and the reason for their acquisition.

The collection has not left Mr. McIlhenny's house often, and it is our great fortune here in Atlanta that he was willing to let us borrow his pictures for more than a third of a year. His family roots in Georgia may have had something to do with it, as well as our pronounced need to show great art at the High Museum. At any rate, the gentle persuasion of Ambassador Anne Cox Chambers and William N. Banks, Mr. McIlhenny's friends, and ours, made these loans possible, something which we deeply appreciate.

We also wish to express our thanks to Richard N. Gregg, Director of the Allentown Museum, who allowed us to use the catalogue texts prepared for the 1977 McIlhenny exhibition in Allentown by his staff— Peter F. Blume and Albertine Désirée Friedman. As on that occasion, Joseph Rishel, Curator of European Painting Before 1900 at the Philadelphia Museum, has provided an illuminating introduction for the catalogue, and, in addition, has written entries for the English paintings which are being presented here for the first time.

We are indebted to Anne d'Harnoncourt, Director of the Philadelphia Museum, for her cooperation and permission to show works donated by Mr. McIlhenny, and likewise to John Rosenfield, Director of the Fogg Art Museum, for agreeing to the loan of the Cézanne watercolor. Mr. McIlhenny's secretary, Katharine Norris, provided us with much information and supervised the arrangements with the photographer Will Brown, who produced all new color transparencies and many black and whites. The High Museum's Registrar, Marjorie Harvey, worked in

Franklin C. Watkins, *Henry P. McIlhenny*, 1941, oil on canvas

close cooperation with Irene Taurins, Registrar of the Philadelphia Museum, to arrange the delicate process of shipping the works from Philadelphia to Atlanta. Eric Zafran, the High Museum's Curator of European Art, coordinated the catalogue and updated the bibliographies and exhibition listings. Kelly Morris of the High Museum's staff edited the catalogue, and Jim Zambounis designed it.

The High Museum is especially grateful to the Directors of National Bank of Georgia for their most generous sponsorship, which brought the collection to Atlanta and made the exhibition and this catalogue possible.

Gudmund Vigtel, Director
High Museum of Art

Introduction

Henry P. McIlhenny's collection of nineteenth century French art is well known through the generous reception scholars and connoisseurs have received from the owner at his house in Philadelphia. Also, there have been frequent exhibitions of some works at the Philadelphia Museum of Art over the years, as well as at The San Francisco Palace of the Legion of Honor (1962), the Allentown Museum (1977), and most recently at the Carnegie Institute, Pittsburgh (1979). Looking back to the first catalogued showing of the works in 1962, it is remarkable to observe how much our understanding of the art of this period has changed.

A reexamination of late eighteenth century aesthetic attitudes in France was initiated in 1964 with the work of Professor Robert Rosenblum and more recently extended through a series of exhibitions held in America and France. Perhaps the most spectacular was the monumental *Age of Revolution* (shown in Paris, Detroit, and New York), which, through the exhibition of some 206 paintings dating from 1774 to 1830, prompted a broad and profound reanalysis of this period. This was preceded by *Le Musée du Luxembourg en 1874* exhibition in Paris in 1974, which reexamined the state of official French taste as seen in the major contemporary public collection. Smaller monographic exhibitions have reconsidered such forgotten figures as Cabanel, Gérôme, Gleyre, Bouguereau and, more recently, Caillebotte, allowing these artists to emerge from seventy or eighty years of obscurity. Exhibitions such as *Art in France During the Second Empire* (Philadelphia, Detroit, and Paris, 1977-78) and *French Salon Paintings from Southern Collections* (Atlanta, Norfolk, Raleigh, and Sarasota, 1983) have built upon this research and extended our enthusiasm. The whole range and variety of nineteenth century French art has been reinforced in its astonishing density and high quality. It was a sweep of creative vitality in the visual arts which, one could argue, was unequaled in any one country in the history of the West.

Yet with all the richness of new material to consider, certain established ideas inherited from critics at the beginning of this century continue to hold. As the number of artists to be seen with pleasure and to be considered worthy of note increase, we continue to return to a common foundation of criticism, a group of artists and specific works whose established value is, as it would have been said in the nineteenth century, "hors concours." Their position of distinction in the history of art has in no way been diminished by a fuller realization of their artistic and social context. In fact, our appreciation of the essential quality of acknowledged masters grows all the greater as our sense of the period becomes more refined.

The earliest painting shown here, and one of the first works acquired by Mr. McIlhenny, is a still life by Jean Siméon Chardin. This artist, justly famous but still little studied, preferred rather unfashionable subjects of still life and genre scenes to the high flown narrative presentations of his exact contemporary, François Boucher. Yet his remarkable directness of vision and simplicity brought him high honor during his lifetime. While harking back to seventeenth century Dutch prototypes, Chardin's matter of fact presentations have a quality of distillation and calm that places him on a quite different plane. His color has all the gentle blondness and clarity of contemporary rococo artists, yet the exclusion of animated or decorative elements and his ability to endow empty space with the same degree of engagement and force as the objects themselves fully justify the comparison to his later admirer, Cézanne.

Something of this quality of detached, sustained observation was to be the governing aesthetic of a group of artists who emerged at the end of the eighteenth century, all trained in Rome but entirely French in their outlook. The foremost figure among this group, which would later be called Neo-Classicist, was Jacques-Louis David, a man of complex personality and high seriousness. Having survived the Revolution and the Reign of Terror, David became the veritable dictator of French art under the rule of Napoleon I.

The McIlhenny collection includes one of David's finest works, the portrait of Pope Pius VII. The Pope, who four years later was to be imprisoned and abused by the Emperor, is depicted at a moment of high pageantry, witnessing the Coronation of Napoleon. This is the repetition of one isolated detail from David's monumental *Coronation of Napoleon*, now in the Louvre. Pius VII sits with grave austerity, carrying all the weight of his office, which would soon be under stormy attack. The presence of his Legate, Cardinal Caprara, protective and wary, creates one of the most profound and probing double portraits in the history of art.

A second masterpiece from this period, dating some seven years later, is Ingres's portrait of the *Comtesse de Tournon*. What he has taken from his master David is clearly evident in his direct perception of his sitter and the essential austerity of his presentation. Yet in his remarkably sensuous and complex use of line and pure, enameled color, Ingres is clearly of the next generation. The full force of Davidian severity has been tempered. His essential kindness to this aging and, one assumes, rather formidable woman is extraordinary, with the wrinkles of her wrist disguised by the paisley shawl and the lace veil. She is grand and secure but with a full sense of comfort and domesticity. Another, more informal aspect of the artist is shown here in a delicate and intimate pencil drawing.

During the next decade, Ingres was to become the most respected and honored artist in France. Unlike David, who was forced into exile at the collapse of the Empire in 1815, Ingres would survive and prosper under three quite different governments until his death in 1867. However, his long career witnessed major aesthetic upheavals within French art, and by the 1820s Ingres found himself, as the primary exponent of the Davidian classical tradition, in violent critical opposition to what we have come to call Romanticism, best shown here in the work of Eugène Delacroix.

In contrast to the *Comtesse de Tournon*, Delacroix's portrait of *Eugène Berny d'Ouville* is loosely and freely painted with little attention to drawn detail. The stern authority of the grand dowager has shifted to a gentle poetic description of wistful youth. Primarily through his interest in English art (he visited that country in 1825 after seeing the work of Constable in Paris), Delacroix wanted to reject the refined draughtsmanship and limited color of the Classicists and pursue a style based on freely brushed paint and broad use of color. Also, in his choice of subjects he stands quite apart from David and Ingres. He was drawn to the exotic, the sensual, and the opulent, and *The Death of Sardanapalus* is perhaps his single most spectacular and operatic work. Color applied with a Venetian complexity was his sustaining interest, as wonderfully evidenced here in an intimate watercolor of a studio wall as in the *Sardanapalus*.

With the exhibition of *Sardanapalus* in 1827, Delacroix became the hero of the Romantics—the primary rallying point for young artists who rejected Ingres. However, one of the surprising things about the dynamic movements within France during the first half of the century is that these stylistic groupings—Classicist vs. Romanticist—shared certain qualities. This is shown in Mr. McIlhenny's collection by two chalk drawings remarkably similar in technique: the male nude of Delacroix, despite its ominous quality of winged darkness, has the same restraint as the more "classical" nude by Prud'hon. The same merging of traditions marks the work of Chassériau, a pupil of Ingres who later became an admirer of Delacroix. His drawing of *Mme. Borg de Balsan* is, in its elegant line and cool dignity, worthy of Ingres, while others of his works have the opulence and exotic allure of Delacroix.

It is often noted that by mid-century the influence of Ingres was on the wane and that the classical tradition had lost its force. Yet in the 1850s an artist emerged who, while entirely distinctive and independent, can be considered the true heir to the tradition: Edgar Degas. The works shown here represent, in diverse ways, the magnitude of his genius, and *Interior* stands as one of the most haunting pictures of the nineteenth century. Degas draws with the refinement and assurance of Ingres and often with the same quality of detached observation. However, his ability to draw with color—especially wonderful in the pastel bather—brings an entirely new aspect to the history of style. This, along with his intensity of observation and detached objectivity, perhaps led to his friendship with the group of artists who first showed together in 1874 and who were later called Impressionists, although few members of this group show Degas's essential austerity.

Renoir's *Mlle. Legrand*, while wonderfully observed and drawn, has a warmth and lushness of execution in marked contrast to Degas. Light, especially its ability to diffuse and divide color, is Renoir's primary subject, as seen here and in the radiant *Les Grands Boulevards* of 1875.

Vincent van Gogh felt much this same desire to observe light and its effect on color but, unlike Renoir (who maintained throughout his long life a positive objectivity about the world around him), van Gogh turned the techniques he learned from the Impressionists to an intensely subjective, highly personal end. *Rain,* his poignant representation of an enclosed field on a cold November day, is permeated with a strange blue and green light, which derives as much from the artist's feelings as from observed fact. The pen drawing of thatched cottages succinctly conveys, even without the addition of color, the quality of the day, while the arching line of the roofs and the lunging perspective create a disconcerting sense of this lonely place.

Three years before his death van Gogh met the young artist Henri de Toulouse-Lautrec, who shared the elder artist's passion for nervous outline and violent color. However, Toulouse-Lautrec's detached sense of observation and subtle draughtsmanship are closer to Degas. The most recent addition to the collection, a drawing of a seated man, is reminiscent of Degas's *M. Plucque.*

The large painting *Au Moulin Rouge* has long been taken as one of the most important French pantings of the 1890s. Many of its characters can be identified and the painting can be read like a droll and analytic novel. These companions of Toulouse-Lautrec's night world are seen in all the lurid colors created by artificial light, unified by an outline of fluid animation.

Impressionism, and by the eighties the extension and reformation of this movement sometimes called Post-Impressionism, included artists of far-ranging styles and temperament. But the figure who stands almost alone—both in terms of essential concerns and his style of painting—is Paul Cézanne. Whereas his sense of observation and objectivity have parallels among many of his colleagues, his quality of observed forms, set and absolute, has its true origin in Chardin more than a century before. It is a vision which has a remarkable uniformity whether his subject is a figure or a landscape. Whereas Renoir, van Gogh, and Toulouse-Lautrec speak to a moment in time, albeit a telling and universal moment, Cézanne seems always to present another world, immutable and still.

This attitude was also to influence the style of a strong admirer of Cézanne in the next generation, Henri Matisse. His *Still Life on a Table* shows ordinary objects lovingly observed in light. Yet with Matisse we are in the twentieth century and the use of color and the adjustment of space are handled in a manner which has taken liberties with direct observation. Just as in the *Study for "The White Plumes,"* not unlike Ingres in its ease and elegant restraints, Matisse has allowed the line a greater independence from its definition of form.

Like his exact contemporary Matisse, Vuillard developed out of the late nineteenth century—and out of Impressionism and Post-Impressionism—but in a distinctly different manner. Here Vuillard's rich and divided colors, as vibrant as Renoir's boulevards, have been applied in a flattened space, creating a dense, rich atmosphere for the tender encounter of the woman and her child.

This dense application of paint in a flattened perspective also marks the work of Georges Rouault, although turned to an entirely different aesthetic end. A fellow student with Matisse in the 1890s, Rouault, after the turn of the century, returned to the memory of his early apprenticeship as a restorer of medieval stained glass from which he drew the somber, highly personal style and religious iconography which sustained him through his life.

In surveying the paintings and drawings in the McIlhenny collection one is struck by how well they relate to each other despite their broad range. Certainly this is so partly because of the remarkably high quality of all the works, and quality was the primary force behind each acquisition. Yet, as happens with private collections of really great distinction, there is an added sense, a sense that far exceeds both their sheer beauty and natural relationships. This, of course, is the outcome of the taste, connoisseurship, and scholarship of the man who gathered the works. It is a truly remarkable achievement.

Yet there is quite another side of Henry McIlhenny's taste which is shown here publicly for the first time. The astonishing group of French nineteenth and early twentieth century paintings and drawings reflect an interest in the profound power and insight of the grand tradition, begun by David and carried through Matisse, which first formulated itself for McIlhenny at the Fogg Museum under the connoisseur and collector Paul Sachs. Yet the Harvard experience provided, almost on the oblique, the beginning of quite another channel of pursuit. While an undergraduate there, McIlhenny met Arthur Kingsley Porter, a scholar of medieval France. Porter and his wife had acquired a nineteenth century shooting place called Glenveagh Castle, in the far north of Ireland in County Donegal. It is a region of vast romantic evocation—a crenelated house of grand proportion beside its own deep, still lake set in a huge barren landscape. McIlhenny visited the Porters there as a student, and the allure of the place stayed with him, perhaps encouraged by the fact that part of his family had originated in this part of Ireland.

Porter disappeared mysteriously near Glenveagh in 1933. The property came onto the market and was purchased by McIlhenny in 1937, although an assignment with the Navy in the South Pacific intervened and he did not actually arrive to properly survey his new summer residence until after the war. At this point he began working on the gardens, which now rank among the most subtly and deliciously varied of any created in this century. McIlhenny also began to stock the house with paintings and objects which he felt appropriate to the place. He was in great luck, if so carefully a chosen group of things can ever be attributed to luck. Victorian pictures were still very much under a cloud. Aided by his innate sense of quality and aptness to the site—even though this leap of taste must have seemed at the time terribly whimsical for a man who had sharpened his eye through the purchase of the consummate Degas drawing or a grand Toulouse-Lautrec—McIlhenny over the next decade and thereafter added a second string to his bow. He collected the English works with as much precision and pleasure as he had shown in his pursuit of French art.

Landseer, particularly the two huge stag pictures, seemed like a natural, especially to anyone who has sat under them at dinner in the castle on a chilly autumn evening and heard the real beasts roaring their mournful challenges across the lake. To these would be added more Landseers, reflecting almost all aspects of his varied and abundant career, as well as other Victorian pictures.

Now that these works have joined the French paintings in Philadelphia, it is striking to what a degree one can see the same mind working in their selection. As diverse as they may seem even to us today, for whom the Channel continues to represent a mighty distance in terms of aesthetic attitudes, they are unified by the one principle which overrides all regional distinctions: quality.

Joseph J. Rishel
Curator of European Painting Before 1900
Philadelphia Museum of Art

Catalogue of the Exhibition

French, numbers 1-41
English, numbers 42-55

Entries on the works were written by Peter F. Blume (P.F.B.), Albertine Désirée Friedman (A.D.F.), and Joseph J. Rishel (J.J.R.). Most of the commentaries on the French works were originally published in slightly longer versions in the 1977 catalogue by the Allentown Art Museum. Dimensions are given height before width before depth.

Jean Siméon Chardin (1699-1779)

1. *The Hare*, ca. 1730

Oil on canvas, 25⅝ x 32 inches

Signed at right center: *Chardin*

Lent by the Philadelphia Museum of Art, gift of Henry P. McIlhenny, retaining life interest.

The Dutch masters of the seventeenth century introduced still-life as a highly sophisticated form of art, using the most common domestic articles as subject matter. Chardin chose to present very few objects in his painting, without deliberately seeking, as the Dutch masters did, an accumulation of textures to show off virtuoso technique. He exploits the subtleties of the modest subject matter with a restricted range of colors and removes himself from his own century's tradition of colorful, aristocratic and artificial hunting trophies. This hare is not a nobleman's prize, but a modest person's possible next meal.

As in his other paintings of these same objects, Chardin does not attempt to create a highly decorative effect. His pyramidal composition, bathed in diffuse light, has a quiet, even majestic dignity. The horizontal and vertical planes are not delineated. Only the curvature of the hare's body indicates the angle.

With unqualified admiration, Diderot wrote about the artist's painstaking creative effort: "Chardin is such a meticulous imitator of nature, such a severe judge of himself, that I saw one of his paintings of hares never finished because the little rabbits from which he was working had begun to rot; he gave up on reaching with other rabbits the harmony he sought. All those that were brought to him were either too brown or too light."[1] Diderot also wrote: "Nobody has a greater understanding of the harmony of color and reflections. Ah, Chardin, what you grind on your palette is . . . the very substance of things. You dip your brush in air and light and spread them on your canvas."[2]

The final result, with its flawless finish, gives no actual indication of Chardin's laborious handling of his impasto. He has completely obliterated his presence: the artist's reality and the spectator's reality are one and the same.

A.D.F.

NOTES

[1]Diderot, *Oeuvres Esthétiques*, Paris, 1965, p. 496.

[2]Ibid., p. 484.

PROVENANCE

M.-F. Dandré-Bardon (sale 1783, no. 7); Laperlier (sales 1867, no. 22 and 1879, no. 3); Baron de Beurnonville (sale 1881, no. 20); Léon Michel-Lévy (sale 1925, no. 128); Wildenstein & Co., New York, 1934.

EXHIBITIONS

Paris, Galerie Martinet, 1860, no. 106; Paris, Musée des Arts Décoratifs, 1880, no. 41; Paris, 1892, no. 6; Paris, 1907, no. 18; New York, Wildenstein Galleries, 1926, no. 9 (repr.); Cambridge, Mass., Fogg Art Museum, 1931; Chicago, 1934, no. 135; New York, Metropolitan Museum of Art, 1935, no. 24 (repr.); Cambridge, Fogg Art Museum, 1936; Philadelphia Museum of Art, 1937; New York World's Fair, 1939, no. 39; Philadelphia Museum of Art, 1949; San Francisco, The California Palace of the Legion of Honor, 1962; Allentown Art Museum, 1977; Paris, Grand Palais, The Cleveland Museum of Art, and Museum of Fine Arts, Boston, 1979, no. 21.

LITERATURE

W. Burger (Thore) in *Gazette des Beaux-Arts*, 1860, p. 334; E. and J. de Goncourt, *L'art du XVIIIe siècle*, 1880, I, p. 189; J. Guiffrey, *Chardin*, 1899, no. 166, p. 83; M. Tourneux in *Gazette des Beaux-Arts*, 38, 1907, p. 95 (repr.); A Dayot and O. Vaillat, *L'oeuvre de J.B.S. Chardin et J.H. Fragonard*, Paris, 1907, no. 47 (repr.); J. Guiffrey, in *Revue de l'Art*, 1907, p. 109; J. Guiffrey, *L'oeuvre de Chardin et Fragonard*, Paris, 1907, p. IX, no. 47 (repr.); J. Guiffrey, *Chardin*, Paris, 1908 (new ed.), no. 166, p. 83; H. Furst, *Chardin*, London, 1911, p. 127; G. Wildenstein, *Chardin*, Paris, 1933, no. 706, fig. 82; Ed. Pilon, *Chardin*, Paris, 1941, p. 35 (repr.); G. Wildenstein, *Chardin*, Zurich, 1963, no. 260; P. Rosenberg, *Chardin 1699-1779*, 1979, pp. 137-138 (repr.).

Pierre-Paul Prud'hon (1758-1823)

2. *Bust of a Female Figure*, ca. 1814

Black chalk, stump, heightened with white chalk on blue-gray paper, 11 x 8⅝ inches

The place of Prud'hon in the art of the nineteenth century is that of the last of the eighteenth century painters. He comes to terms neither with David's strict classicism, nor with the robust adventure of the Romantics. His art is a curious hybrid, the elements of which are visible here.

The model's torso is illuminated by a direct overhead light source which defines the full volume of the breasts and even provides the subtle description of the surface anatomy; she raises her arm to shadow her face in the misty *sfumato* of Correggio. Small drawings such as this are Prud'hon's most successful accomplishments.

P.F.B.

PROVENANCE
His de la Salle; Henriquel Dupont; Eugène Laporte, 1937

EXHIBITIONS
Paris, Ecole des Beaux-Arts, 1874, no. 429; Paris, Petit Palais, 1922, no. 218, p. 42; London, Royal Academy of Arts, 1932, no. 866 (repr.); Paris, Palais National des Arts, 1937, no. 710; Philadelphia Museum of Art, 1947, no. 109; Philadelphia Museum of Art, 1949; Cambridge, Mass., Fogg Art Museum, 1958; San Francisco, The California Palace of the Legion of Honor, 1962; Allentown Art Museum, 1977; Pittsburgh, Carnegie Institute, 1979.

LITERATURE
Ch. Clément, *Prud'hon*, Paris, 1872, p. 392; E. de Goncourt, *Catalogue de l'oeuvre de Prud'hon*, Paris, 1876, p. 297, no. 190 (as "Marguerite"); C. Martine and L. Marotte, "Pierre-Paul Prud'hon," *Dessins des maîtres français*, III, Paris, 1923, no. 63; J. Guiffrey, *Oeuvre de Prud'hon*, Paris, 1924, p. 431, no. 1116; E. Gradmann, *French Master Drawings of the Eighteenth Century*, New York, 1949, no. 53 (repr.); R. Schoolman and C. E. Slatkin, *Six Centuries of French Master Drawings in America*, New York, 1950, p. 61.

Jacques-Louis David (1748-1825)

3. *Pope Pius VII and Cardinal Caprara*, ca. 1805

Oil on panel, 54⅜ x 37¾ inches

Signed at bottom center: *L. David*

Inscribed at top: *PIE VII A L'AGE DE 63 ANS/LE C^{nal} CAPRARA, SON LEGAT EN FRANCE*

Lent by the Philadelphia Museum of Art, partial gift of Henry P. McIlhenny.

Pius VII was sixty-three when he went to Paris at Napoleon's behest to bestow an air of legitimacy on the newly-founded Empire. He went, against the advice of his council, to seek a *modus vivendi* between the Church and Napoleon. Cardinal Caprara was hand-picked by Napoleon as the Papal Legate in France; he was a pawn of the state in a country where the prestige of the Church had been shattered since the Revolution sixteen years before.

The portraits are extracted from David's monumental *Coronation of Napoleon (Le Sacre)*, a vast surface of 476 square feet, containing over one hundred individual portraits. The huge painting was an important part of Napoleon's propaganda machine, for the Pope's benediction is Napoleon's link with established ecclesiastical authority and was a detail altered to suit the new Emperor. David originally conceived the Pope with his hands resting on his thighs in total resignation, while Napoleon all but prances about with the crown in his hands.

In the insightful double portrait, David has intensified the light source from the upper left. The two prelates are now projected in an infinite space, removed from the crowd scene. Cardinal Caprara is soft, complacent, perhaps somewhat sinister in his passivity. Pope Pius VII's character is charged by the noble simplicity of his gesture; his posture is resigned but his face is intelligent. Even the drape of his vestments, in contrast to the cardinal's soft ermine, has a linear electricity.

P.F.B.

PROVENANCE

Sold by David to Firmin Didot; Jacques Lafitte (sale, 1834); Pourtalès (sale, 1865, no. 241); Earl Dudley (sale, 1892, no. 37); Marquise de Ganay (sale, 1922, no. 39, repr.); Lasquin, Marquis de Ganay, 1937.

EXHIBITIONS

Leeds, 1868, no. 2915; London, Royal Academy of Arts, Winter Exhibition, 1871, no. 362; Paris, Palais des Beaux-Arts, 1913, no. 41; London, Royal Academy of Arts, 1932, no. 337, pl. 82; Philadelphia, Museum of Art, 1937; Pennsylvania, Bryn Mawr College, 1940; New York, Metropolitan Museum of Art, 1941, no. 32, fig. 3; New York, The Century Association, 1947, no. 16 (repr.); Philadelphia Museum of Art, 1947, no. 2 (repr.); Philadelphia Museum of Art, 1949; San Francisco, The California Palace of the Legion of Honor, 1962; Philadelphia Museum of Art, 1977; Allentown Art Museum, 1977; Pittsburgh, Carnegie Institute, 1979.

LITERATURE

P. Mantz, "La galerie Pourtalès," *Gazette des Beaux-Arts*, Feb., 1865, pp. 114-16 (repr.); J. David, *Le peintre L. David*, 1880, p. 645; C. Dreyfus, in *Les Arts*, 1909, no. 96, p. 25 (repr.); R. Cantinelli, *David*, Paris, 1930, no. 116, pl. LXII; P. Jamot, "French Painting-II," *The Burlington Magazine*, 60, Jan., 1932, pl. XXVIII; R. Verbraeken, *Jacques-Louis David jugé par ses contemporains et par la postérité*, Paris, 1973, p. 106, pl. 50; D. and G. Wildenstein, *Documents complémentaires au catalogue de l'oeuvre de Louis David*, Paris, 1973, p. 165; A. Schnapper, *David*, New York, 1982, p. 245 (repr. in color).

PIE VII
A L'AGE DE 63 ANS.
LE C.NAL CAPRARA
SON LÉGAT EN FRANCE

Attributed to François-Xavier Fabre (1766-1837)

4. *Portrait of Ugo Foscolo*

Oil on canvas, 25½ x 21 inches

Undeciphered monogram at lower left

This haunting portrait has perplexed scholars for some time. It is obviously by a very strong painter somewhat under the influence of Jacques-Louis David, an artist whose name is often attached to a large group of classical-romantic portraits which extend far beyond his immediate circle either in France or Italy. Recently, by great good fortune, James Lord (as reported in correspondence with the owner) has come across a drawing in the Musée Marmottan in Paris which sheds considerable new light on the problem. The drawing by Francois-Xavier Fabre depicts the celebrated Italian poet Ugo Foscolo and bears a striking resemblance to the McIlhenny picture.

A member of David's studio in Paris, Fabre won the Prix de Rome and, like several of his fellow students at the French Academy in Rome, was stranded there by the French Revolution, which both cut off his stipend and prevented his return. Intense anti-French sentiments erupted in Rome in 1793, when Louis XVI was executed, and Fabre beat a retreat to Florence, where he was protected and patronized by two remarkable expatriate women: the Countess of Albany, widow of the second-to-last Stuart pretenter, and Lady Holland. From this vantage, he witnessed and emotionally rode out the storm of the momentous political events then changing all of Europe. The poet Vittorio Alfieri was the spiritual leader of this group; he was also the Countess's lover after the death of James Edward Stuart.

In 1813, the group was joined by Ugo Foscolo (1778-1827), a playwright, essayist and poet who embodied in his life and work much of the social drama and inner torment which Italy was going through at that point. Having initially applauded the Napoleonic invasion of the northern section of the peninsula, he fell into deep disillusionment with the Treaty of Campo Formio, at which Napoleon handed over the Veneto (1797) to the Austrians. Like a figure out of Stendhal, Foscolo vacillated between international republican sentiments and his own growing passion for an Italian nation. He was at the peak of his fame when he was forced to retreat from Milan to Florence in 1813. His stay was short-lived and he returned to Milan the same year. With the arrival of Austrian troops, he fled to Switzerland and eventually to England (1816) where he remained until his death. His reputation in Italy is perhaps most clearly revealed by the fact that forty-four years after his death—in 1871, the year of the political unification of Italy—his remains were transported to Florence and placed in Santa Croce, the new Italian pantheon, alongside Machiavelli, Alfieri, Michelangelo, and Galileo.

Two portraits by Fabre, both from 1813, are already known: one is in the collection of the National Library, Florence, signed and dated 1813 (given by Conte Sen. Antonio Cippico, who bought it in London, Sotheby's, 15 May, 1929); the other, unsigned and with small variations, was formerly in the collection of Mario Praz (purchased London, Christie's, 1938). Praz notes that Garagalli, encouraged by Foscolo, made several copies. The McIlhenny picture, which is markedly different from the Praz/Florence type, is clearly as high in quality. We must await Lord's further research to fully establish the identity of the sitter and, one hopes, to decipher the enigmatic monogram on the lower left.

J.J.R.

PROVENANCE

Maurice Rheims, Paris; Wildenstein Gallery, New York.

EXHIBITIONS

San Francisco, The California Palace of the Legion of Honor, 1962; Allentown Art Museum, 1977; Pittsburgh, Carnegie Institute, 1979.

LITERATURE

Mostra Foscoliana, Florence, Biblioteca Nazionale Centrale, 1939, frontispiece and p. 38; M. Praz (trans. A. Davidson), *The House of Life*, New York, 1964, pp. 322-324 and colorplate C; *French Painting: 1774-1830: The Age of Revolution*, New York, Metropolitan Museum of Art, 1973, pp. 410-411.

Jean Auguste Dominique Ingres (1780-1867)

5. *Portrait of a Man*, 1811

Pencil on white paper, 8 x 6 inches

Signed and dated at bottom left: *Ingres Rome/ 1811*

Stamp of the collection of François Flameng at bottom right (Lugt, no. 991)

There are about three hundred of these acute portrait studies done by Ingres when he was in Rome between 1806 and 1820. Lapauze's identification of this man as the critic Gustav Jal has recently been disputed by Neef.

Compared to other Ingres drawings of this type, this small work is relatively unfinished, which may suggest an easy informality between the artist and sitter. The costume is deftly indicated but not worked in any detail; the hair remains a series of short strokes of the pencil, contributing to the rather surprised expression. It is the incisive quality of the line, however, which influenced Chassériau and, later, Degas.

P.F.B.

EXHIBITIONS

Paris, Georges Petit Galleries, 1911; Cambridge, Mass., Fogg Art Museum, 1934; New York, M. Knoedler Galleries (etc.), 1940, no. 37; Philadelphia Museum of Art, 1947, no. 108; Philadelphia Museum of Art, 1949; Cambridge, Fogg Art Museum, 1958; San Francisco, The California Palace of the Legion of Honor, 1962; Allentown Art Museum, 1977; Pittsburgh, Carnegie Institute, 1979.

LITERATURE

H. Lapauze, *Ingres*, Paris, 1911, p. 100 (repr.); H. Neef, *Die Bildniszeichnungen von J.-A.-D. Ingres*, Bern, 1977, IV, pp. 128-129, no. 68 (repr.).

Jean Auguste Dominique Ingres (1780-1867)

6. *La Comtesse de Tournon*, 1812

Oil on canvas, 36⅝ x 28¾ inches

Signed and dated at right: *Ingres Rome/1812*

In his only portrait of an older woman, Ingres has portrayed the character of the Comtesse de Tournon in the style of David, putting us into direct confrontation with the sitter. The Comtesse was the mother of the Préfet de Rome, the baron Camille de Tournon, who commissioned this portrait.

However slightly inclined towards characterization, Ingres appears to have given us, at first glance, the bare facts. But as Robert Rosenblum has noted,[1] and Lapauze before him,[2] it is a carefully constructed artifice around a woman who was never a beauty, and past her prime at that. The hair is probably a wig; any possibility of a double chin has been camouflaged by a large ruff; and while the arms are exposed, her fingers are gracefully concealed for the most part in the smooth velvet of the gown and the exotically fashionable cashmere shawl. In her face, there are no wrinkles, but we detect a slightly sunken mouth and the possibility of a problem with the teeth behind. Clearly, Ingres has gone to great pains to portray our sitter in her best light; she is radiant, alive, and undoubtedly a formidable presence in any *salon*.

The fugue played by the lines of the carefully arranged fabrics serves to direct our attention to that remarkable face: the lace winds to a tight halo around the head; the green velvet culminates at the more relaxed roundish puff of the sleeve; and the shawl flows into a cascade over the arm of the chair.

P.F.B.

NOTES

[1]Robert Rosenblum, *Ingres*, New York, 1967, p. 92.
[2]H. Lapauze, *Ingres*, Paris, 1911, pp. 114-118.

PROVENANCE

Comte de Tournon; Marquis de Tournon; Comte Jean de Chabannes-la-Palice; Paul Rosenberg, Paris, 1935.

EXHIBITIONS

Paris, 1867, no. 581; Paris, Georges Petit Galleries, 1911, no. 19; Paris, Hôtel de la Chambre Syndicale de la Curiosité et des Beaux-Arts, 1921, no. 18 (repr.); Paris, rue de la Ville l'Évêque, 1924, no. 18 (repr.); Cambridge, Mass., Fogg Art Museum, 1936; Philadelphia Museum of Art, 1937; New York, Metropolitan Museum of Art, 1941, no. 72 (repr.); Philadelphia Museum of Art, 1947, no. 2 (repr.); Paris, Musée de l'Orangerie, 1955, no. 36 (repr.); San Francisco, The California Palace of the Legion of Honor, 1962; Allentown Art Museum, 1977; Pittsburgh, Carnegie Institute, 1979.

LITERATURE

H. Delaborde, *Ingres, sa vie et ses travaux*, Paris, 1870, no. 157; H. Lapauze, *Ingres*, Paris, 1911, pp. 114-118, 121 (repr.); L. Frölich-Bume, *Ingres*, London, 1926, p. 10, pl. 19; W. Pach, *Ingres*, New York, 1939, pp. 44, 136; *Art Digest*, 23, July 1, 1949, p. 7 (repr.); W. Friedlaender, *David to Delacroix*, Cambridge, 1952, p. 79, fig. 44; G. Wildenstein, *Ingres*, New York, 1954, no. 84, pl. 27; R. Rosenblum, *Jean Auguste Dominique Ingres*, New York, n. d. [1967], p. 92, pl. 19 (repr.); J. Whiteley, *Ingres*, London, 1977, p. 41, pl. 24.

Théodore Chassériau (1819-1856)

7. *Mme. Borg de Balsan*, 1847

Pencil on white paper, 13⅛ x 10⅝ inches

Signed and dated at bottom left: *Théodore Chassériau / 1847*

Chassériau's portraits are distinguished, as John S. Newberry, Jr., has observed, "by their penetrating characterization, an appealing nostalgic sensitivity and a searching realism which is tempered by classical repose and aristocratic taste."[1] All of these qualities are present in this portrait of Mme. Borg de Balsan and we can see the profound influence of his master, Ingres. Newberry continues: "The drawing of the head is in contrast to the free sketching of the costume, which is here softer and less precise than in drawings by Ingres."[2]

This freedom from Ingres's precision is still in its experimental stage here, and the full range of Chassériau's gifts was not exhibited until he came under the spell of Delacroix's romanticism.

P.F.B.

NOTES

[1]A. Mongan, ed., *One Hundred Master Drawings*, Cambridge, Mass., 1949, p. 154.

[2]Ibid.

PROVENANCE

Thomson, Versailles; Wildenstein & Co., New York, 1935.

EXHIBITIONS

Paris, Musée de l'Orangerie, 1933, no. 130; Cambridge, Mass., Fogg Art Museum, 1936; Cambridge, Fogg Art Museum, 1946; Philadelphia Museum of Art, 1947, no. 113; Philadelphia Museum of Art, 1950-51, no. 84 (repr.); Paris, Musée de l'Orangerie, 1955, no. 60 (repr.); Cambridge, Fogg Art Museum, 1958; San Francisco, The California Palace of the Legion of Honor, 1962; Allentown Art Museum, 1977; Pittsburgh, Carnegie Institute, 1979.

LITERATURE

L. Bénédite, *Théodore Chassériau, sa vie et son oeuvre*, Paris, 1932, II, p. 350; A. Mongan, ed., *One Hundred Master Drawings*, Cambridge, 1949, p. 154 (repr.); Marc Sandoz, *Théodore Chassériau, Catalogue Raisonné des peintures et estampes*, Paris, 1974, p. 13.

Eugène Delacroix (1798-1863)

8. *The Fireplace*, 1824

Watercolor on paper, 6½ x 8¾ inches
Stamp of Vente Delacroix at right

This homely scene of a hearth seems quite out of place in Delacroix's oeuvre. The entry in his *Journal* for January 4, 1824 reads: "Poor devil! Who can create amid these everlasting links with all that is vulgar? Think of the great Michelangelo. Feed yourself on grand and severe ideas of beauty which feed the soul. I am ever turned from the study by foolish distractions."[1] No "grand and severe ideas" here.

This early phase of Delacroix's career was influenced not only by his association with his English friends, Thales and Copley Fielding, but also by Richard Parkes Bonington, his fellow in the studio of Guérin. The simplicity of the subject and the transparent watercolor technique here suggest these English influences, but the sparkling color that is Delacroix's greatest achievement is clearly already his own.

P.F.B.

NOTES

[1]W. Pach, trans., *The Journal of Eugène Delacroix*, New York, 1937.

PROVENANCE

Delacroix (sale, 1864, part no. 658); Dutilleux (sale, 1874, no. 16); Henri Rouart (sale II, 1912, no. 81, as *"Intérieur"*); Jacques Seligmann & Co., New York.

EXHIBITIONS

Philadelphia Museum of Art, 1949; Cambridge, Mass., Fogg Art Museum, 1958; San Francisco, The California Palace of the Legion of Honor, 1962; Allentown Art Museum, 1977; Pittsburgh, Carnegie Institute, 1979.

LITERATURE

A. Robaut, *L'oeuvre complète de Eugène Delacroix*, Paris, 1885, no. 90, p. 29; R. Escholier, *Delacroix*, Paris, 1926, I, repr. (in color) op. p. 80.

Eugène Delacroix (1798-1863)

9. *Eugène Berny d'Ouville*, 1828

Oil on canvas, 24 x 19¾ inches

Signed and dated at lower right: *Eug. Delacroix/1828*

This is one of a series of about ten portraits commissioned by M. Goubaux, principal of the Institution St. Victor, a private, very selective secondary school. Delacroix was well paid for each of these early portraits, done between 1828 and 1834. It is the same period in which his first great machines, *The Bark of Dante*, *Massacre at Scio*, and *The Death of Sardanapalus* were presented to the Salons of 1822, 1824, and 1827, respectively, to great if controversial acclaim. Escholier dissociates this portrait from the other nine, commenting: "Let's completely set aside the charming portrait of Eugène Berny d'Ouville, having such a delicate expression, such a supple finish. The light rose cravat and the pale yellow vest add a youthful, cheery touch to the olive-brown frock coat, a 'smoking ruins' brown indeed."[1]

The gaze scanning the faraway distance, the melancholy expression, and the fashionably pale face are unmistakably romantic, yet they do not betray a contrived pose, as do many such portraits. Youth, sensitivity, and the bright clothes avoid the Byronesque doom inherent in the "smoking ruins" brown. There is a dreamy quality about the portrait created primarily through the softened contours and the careful blending of the hues. The sitter remains in his own world, refusing a rapport with the viewer.

A.D.F.

NOTES

[1]R. Escholier, *Delacroix*, Paris, 1926, I, p. 251, repr. 253.

PROVENANCE

Arosa; Dr. George Viau; Jacques Seligmann & Co., New York, 1933.

EXHIBITIONS

Paris, Hôtel Charpentier, 1926; Paris, Maison de Victor Hugo, 1927, no. 276; Paris, Musée du Louvre, 1930, no. 47 (repr.); Cambridge, Mass., Fogg Art Museum, 1934; Philadelphia Museum of Art, 1937; Hartford, Wadsworth Atheneum, 1952, no. 28 (repr.); Philadelphia, Jane Harper Galleries, Alliance Française, 1958; San Francisco, The California Palace of the Legion of Honor, 1962; Cleveland Museum of Art, 1963; Allentown Art Museum, 1977; Pittsburgh, Carnegie Institute, 1979.

LITERATURE

A. Robaut, *L'oeuvre complète de Eugène Delacroix*, Paris, 1885, no. 257, p. 73; R. Escholier, *Delacroix*, Paris, 1926, I, p. 251, repr. p. 253; W. George, "Genèse d'une crise," *L'Amour de l'Art*, Sept., 1932, pp. 268-69, repr. p. 271; L. Johnson, *The Paintings of Eugène Delacroix, A Critical Catalogue 1816-1831*, Oxford, 1981, I, pp. 49-50, no. 75, II, pl. 66 (repr.).

Eugène Delacroix (1798-1863)

10. *The Death of Sardanapalus*, 1844

Oil on canvas, 29⅛ x 36⅝ inches

This painting is a small-scale reprise of a work with the same title exhibited in the Salon of 1827-1828, where it was received with vitriolic criticism. The classicists were offended by the apparently chaotic assembly of men, women, animals and worldly possessions; the romantics were appalled not by the confusion but by what they found to be an excess of calculation in both composition and mannered detail. In discussing the two versions, John Canaday argues that in the first, "the total effect, while gorgeous, is more gorgeous than passionate . . . the remarkable thing about the late version is that . . . it has all the effect of spontaneous emotional fervor" despite the interim period of seventeen years.[1]

The second supplement to the Catalogue of the Salon of 1827-1828 presents Delacroix's own description of the event: "The rebels besiege Sardanapalus in his palace. Reclining on the superb bed at the summit of an immense pyre, Sardanapalus gives the order to his eunuchs and the palace officers to slaughter his women, his pages, even his horses and his favorite dogs, so that nothing that had served his pleasure might survive him. . . . Aischeh, a Bactrican woman, not wishing to be put to death by a slave, hanged herself from one of the columns supporting the vaulted ceiling. Sardanapalus's cupbearer, Baleah, finally committed the pyre to flame and threw himself upon it."[2]

While Sardanapalus, the archetypal romantic hero, was tormented in life, he is calm and serene before his imminent suicide. Pausing only for the execution of his orders, the King will drink poison from the chalice at his right. Dying, in this painting, is not a passive process.

The principal differences between the large version and the reprise are the size and brushwork. The reduced scale works in favor of the composition by concentrating the action, and the direct application of paint sacrifices fussy detail in favor of the canvas's spontaneous movement. Delacroix has also strengthened the complicated diagonal composition by reinforcing with color the spiral that revolves around it: the licks of flame in the smoky upper right section are significant additions in this regard.

While the generally acknowledged source of inspiration for Delacroix's painting is Byron's dramatic poem *Sardanapalus*, published in 1821, recent scholarship indicates there may be additional contemporary and classical sources influencing Delacroix.[3] F. A. Trapp concludes that the romantic creative process was by no means an improvisation, but the result of strenuous research.[4] This strenuous research pertains not only to iconography, but to the aesthetic problems in the first version. His return to the subject is also indicative of the tenacity with which he pursued specific goals. The reprise is the culmination of seventeen years' experience. Most significantly, the 1832 trip to Morocco provided the raw essence of Orientalism that replaced the story book phantasmagoria of detail found in the first version.

A.D.F.

NOTES:

[1]J. Canady, *Mainstreams of Modern Art*, New York, 1959, p. 49.
[2]Quoted in F. A. Trapp, *The Attainment of Delacroix*, Baltimore, 1971, p. 84.
[3]B. Farwell, "Sources of Delacroix's Death of Sardanapalus," *The Art Bulletin*, XL, March 1958, pp. 66-71; L. Johnson, "The Etruscan Sources of Delacroix's Death of Sardanapalus," *The Art Bulletin*, XLII, Dec., 1960, pp. 297-298.
[4]Trapp, *op. cit.*, pp. 83-92.

PROVENANCE

Legrand; Crabbe, Brussels; Bellino; Paul Rosenberg, Paris.

EXHIBITIONS

New York, Wildenstein Galleries, 1944, no. 18 (repr.); Philadelphia Museum of Art, 1947, no. 4; Philadelphia Museum of Art, 1949; Philadelphia Museum of Art, 1950-51, no. 52 (repr.); San Francisco, The California Palace of the Legion of Honor, 1962; Philadelphia Museum of Art, 1970; Allentown Art Museum, 1977; Pittsburgh, Carnegie Institute, 1979; Rochester, 1982, no. 27.

LITERATURE

A. Robaut, *L'oeuvre complète de Eugène Delacroix*, Paris, 1885, no. 791; *Art Digest*, II, Apr. 1, 1937, p. 8 (repr.); E. Porada, "The Assyrians in the Last Hundred Years," *Bulletin of the Metropolitan Museum of Art*, 4, Summer, 1945, p. 39 (repr.); W. Friedlaender, *David to Delacroix*, Cambridge, 1952, pp. 112-113, fig. 71; R. Huyghe, "Delacroix and Baudelaire," *Arts Yearbook II*, 1958, p. 23 (repr.); F. A. Trapp, *The Attainment of Delacroix*, Baltimore, 1970, p. 92; J. J. Spector, *Delacroix: The Death of Sardanapalus*, London, 1974, pp. 43-44, repr. p. 102; L. Johnson, *The Paintings of Eugène Delacroix, A Critical Catalogue 1816-1831*, Oxford, 1981, I, p. 116; D. Rosenthal, *Orientalism*, Rochester, 1982, p. 32, fig. 22 (repr. in color).

Eugène Delacroix (1798-1863)

11. *Allegorical Figure of Envy (Le Génie ou L'Envie)*, 1849?

Black chalk, 19 x 16¼ inches

Atelier stamp at lower center and right: *E. D.*

There is a brooding sensuality to this strangely androgynous figure that places it in the context of a larger scheme. The suggestion of large wings further complicates his identity and removes him from a terrestrial mode, even though the studio support of his left hand is still visible.

Part of the entry in Delacroix's *Journal* for Friday, May 16, 1823, reads: "Don't forget the allegory of the Man of Genius at the portals of the tomb. . . ."[1] This is the first of the entries in his *Journal* citing a grand allegorical composition of the above subject. Such notations continued as late as 1854. Sérullaz has tentatively dated related drawings 1849 (Metropolitan Museum of Art 61.160.0 and Louvre RF9 933 and RF9 362).[2] McIlhenny's single figure is the most finished of these drawings. Less finished, but unmistakably the same, this winged figure appears in a drawing titled *Le Génie, ou L'Envie* (RF9 362) at the right of a Dantesque figure representing "Genius in the Arms of Glory." Although the juxtaposition of the two figures is by no means certain in the Louvre drawing, Sérullaz's identification of the winged figure among "Les Mauvais Génies" (the evil spirits) is correct. This figure's languorous posture and brooding expression prompt its identification as envy. The most startling difference between the two drawings is the size and shape of the wings. They have grown from the small zephyr-like shape and position in the Louvre drawing to a Daedalian proportion here.

The drawing is among the finest in Delacroix's oeuvre, showing a masterful command of academic anatomy in a provocative and romantic subject.

P.F.B.

NOTES

[1]*The Journal of Eugène Delacroix*, W. Pach, trans., New York, 1937, p. 49.

[2]M. Sérullaz, *Exposition Eugène Delacroix*, Paris, 1963, p. 221.

PROVENANCE

Henri Rouart, Paris, (2nd Sale, December 16-18, 1912, no. 135), Wildenstein, 1970.

EXHIBITIONS

Allentown Art Museum, 1977; Pittsburgh, Carnegie Institute, 1979.

LITERATURE

A. Alexandre, *La Collection Henri Rouart*, Paris, 1912, p. 143.

Constantin Guys (1805-1892)
12. *Military Scene*

Pen and watercolor on white paper,
5 x 9⅜ inches

One of the most popular illustrators of the century, Constantin Guys was a war correspondent for the *Illustrated London News*. In this capacity, he covered the Revolution of 1848 and the Crimean War. He served as a dragoon in the French army and was a veteran of the Greek War of Independence. The *Military Scene* is one of numerous sketches reproduced through wood engraving in the journals of the Second Empire as a means of illustrating current events.

This work demonstrates the use of minimal detail to recreate the ambience of a specific occurrence. Once the figure of a grenadier on a horse is clearly defined in the foreground, the rounded, well-aligned shadows to the right are sufficient to identify the typical fur hats of the entire grenadier guard. The minute vertical lines above them suggest the rifles at attention, just as the silhouettes of the bicorn hats on the left identify the group of *polytechniciens*, officers who graduated from the Ecole Polytechnique. With a mere interplay of shadow and a minimal number of ingeniously chosen details, Guys is thus able to suggest a large military crowd and to convey a sense of immediacy and movement.

A.D.F.

PROVENANCE
Claude Roger-Marx, Paris.

EXHIBITIONS
Philadelphia Museum of Art, 1949; San Francisco, The California Palace of the Legion of Honor, 1962; Allentown Art Museum, 1977; Pittsburgh, Carnegie Institute, 1979.

LITERATURE
P. G. Konody, *The Painter of Victorian Life*, London, 1930, p. 91 (repr.).

Camille Corot (1796-1875)

13. *The Aqueduct (Aqueducs dans la Campagne Romaine)*, ca. 1826-28

Oil on canvas, 9½ x 17¼ inches

Stamp of the Vente Corot at bottom right

Never intended for exhibition, the small studies of the Roman *campagna* done during Corot's stay in Italy between 1825 and 1828 were intended by the artist as preliminary studies to be worked into larger, more formal compositions of classical landscape. We have come to regard them as small masterpieces, and precursors to the Impressionists in the truth of the tonal range they record.

In *The Aqueduct*, Corot has reduced all textural variation to broad masses of light and shade, creating a landscape of timeless solidity.

P.F.B.

PROVENANCE

Corot (sale, May 26, 1875, no. 11); Henri Rouart (sale, I, Dec. 9-11, 1912, no. 109, repr. op. p. 76); Lord Berners, London.

EXHIBITIONS

Allentown Art Museum, 1977; Pittsburgh, Carnegie Institute, 1979.

LITERATURE

A. Robaut and E. Moreau-Nélaton, *L'oeuvre de Corot*, Paris, 1905, II, p. 30, no. 74, 31 (repr.); E. Faure, *Corot*, Paris, 1931, no. 7 (repr.).

Camille Corot (1796-1875)

14. *Study of a Standing Female Nude*, ca. 1845-50

Pencil on cream-colored paper, 18 x 9 inches

Stamp of the Vente Corot at bottom left; the number 176 at top left, lined through

This monumental figure of a woman, convincing in her solidity and yet graceful and light in her movement, is far from the graceless realism and weightiness of Courbet's nudes. The model has her arms crossed above her breasts, and conceals the lower part of her face—though she is not for an instant immodest, there is a certain coyness of expression. The figure is frank and carefully contained by line, but softly modeled and feminine. There is none of the brooding sentimentality that we often find in the classically monumental female figures of Corot's late career.

P.F.B.

PROVENANCE

Corot (sale, 1875, part no. 554); Henri Rouart (sale, II, 1912, no. 18 repr.); Paul Rosenberg, Paris, 1933.

EXHIBITIONS

Paris, Exposition Universelle, 1889, no. 122; Paris, Exposition Universelle, 1900, no. 831; Cambridge, Mass., Fogg Art Museum, 1934, no. 4; Northampton, Mass., Smith College Museum of Art, 1934; Buffalo, Albright Art Gallery, 1935, no. 98 (repr.); Cambridge, Fogg Art Museum, 1936; Philadelphia Museum of Art, 1946, no. 83 (repr.); San Francisco, The California Palace of the Legion of Honor, 1947, no. 40 (repr.); Philadelphia Museum of Art, 1947, no. 115; Philadelphia Museum of Art, 1949; Paris, Musée de l'Orangerie, 1955, no. 63, pl. 21; Cambridge, Fogg Art Museum, 1958; San Francisco, The California Palace of the Legion of Honor, 1962; Allentown Art Museum, 1977; Pittsburgh, Carnegie Institute, 1979.

LITERATURE

A. Robaut and E. Moreau-Nélaton, *L'oeuvre de Corot*, Paris, 1905, IV, no. 2867; *ibid.*, I, p. 114 (repr.); René-Jean, *Corot*, Le Musée Ancien, Paris, 1931, pl. LX.

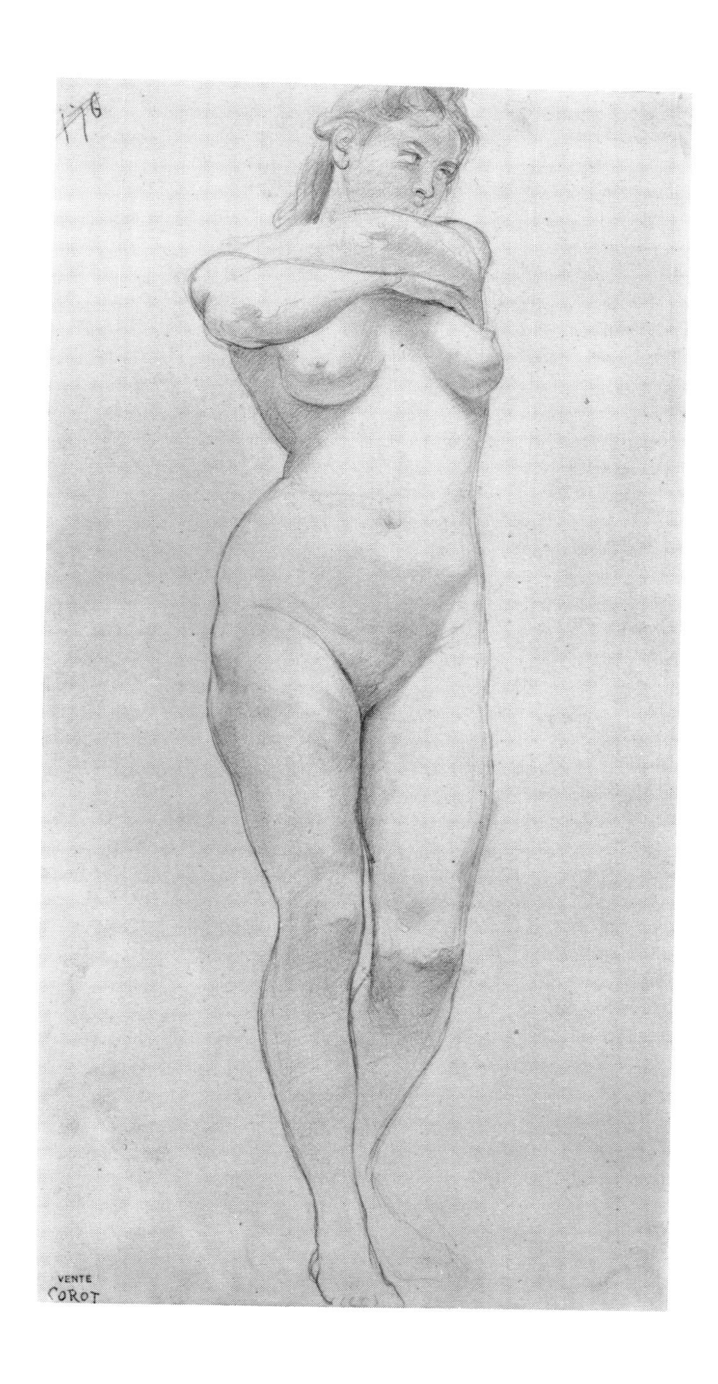
170
VENTE
COROT

Gustav Courbet (1819-1877)

15. *Zélie*, ca. 1850

Crayon and wash on paper, 12¾ x 8 inches
Signed at bottom right: *G. Courbet*

Zélie, the artist's middle sister, was by no means a beautiful woman. There is no attempt on the part of Courbet to embellish her appearance. Although a loving brother, he remains above all a realist. Dressed in her Sunday best, Zélie's attire is provincial, the hairdo self-inflicted and unbecoming. She is unrefined, yet her direct expressive eyes, the discreet shadows pulling downward, convey a sense of shy introspection, of melancholy, which makes her instantly appealing. She is a woman for whom one might feel an affection, but never a delight in the sparkle of her company.

A.D.F.

PROVENANCE
Émile Bernard, Paris; Wildenstein & Co., London, 1961.

EXHIBITIONS
Caracas, 1957, no. 26; London, Wildenstein & Co., 1960, no. 60; San Francisco, The California Palace of the Legion of Honor, 1962; Allentown Art Museum, 1977; Pittsburgh, Carnegie Institute, 1979.

Honoré Daumier (1808-1879)

16. *Ratapoil*, after the plaster executed in 1851

Bronze, 17½ inches high

Inscribed back of base at top left: *3/20*; at bottom right: *Alexis Rudier/Fondeur-Paris*

In the middle of the nineteenth century, *Ratapoil* was not just a hilarious-looking statuette. For millions of Frenchmen it was the embodiment of the corrupt dictatorship of Napoleon III. Elected to the presidency in 1848, Prince Louis Napoleon created a powerful and ruthless police system which deftly orchestrated his coup d'état of 1851, marking the advent of the Second Empire. A staunch partisan of a democratic republic and a supremely witty cartoonist, Daumier used his skills to alert the French people of the impending dictatorship, while elevating caricature to a superior artistic level. Daumier created clay figures as three-dimensional points of reference for a series of caricatures. Not only was Ratapoil (translated from the French as "the hairy rat") the subject of numerous Daumier cartoons, but other writers and cartoonists adopted him and used him in their works. Ratapoil became a constant reminder of the regime's wrongdoings, and was in time considered a "public enemy" by the authorities. Wary of confiscation, Mme. Daumier had constantly to change its hiding place.[1] Jules Michelet, on seeing the statuette in his friend's studio, exclaimed, "Ah, You have hit the enemy directly. Behold the Napoleonic idea forever pilloried!"[2]

The discrepancy between the self-conscious swagger of the pose and the poor fit of his rumpled clothes and hat contribute to his ridiculous aspect, aptly emphasized by the freely modeled bronze surface. A closer look reveals a menacing facial expression. Oliver Larkin contends it is not Louis Napoleon who is embodied here: "It was the intrigue and not the intriguer for whom he had found a symbol in the shoddy Ratapoil."[3]

A.D.F.

NOTES

[1]R. Escholier, *Daumier et son monde*, Editions Berger-Levrault, Paris, 1965, p. 86.

[2]O. W. Larkin, *Daumier: Man of His Time*, London, 1967, p. 106.

[3]Ibid., p. 107.

PROVENANCE

Adolph Lewisohn, New York.

EXHIBITIONS

Cambridge, Mass., Fogg Art Museum, 1958; San Francisco, The California Palace of the Legion of Honor, 1962; Allentown Art Museum, 1977; Pittsburgh, Carnegie Institute, 1979.

LITERATURE

L. Benoist, *La sculpture romantique*, p. 143; H. Marcel, *Honoré Daumier*, n.d., p. 119 (repr.); A. Alexandre, *Honoré Daumier*, Paris, 1888, pp. 295 ff., 379 (repr., the plaster); G. Geffroy, in *L'Art et les Artistes*, 1905, p. 108 (repr.); J. Meier-Graefe, *Modern Art*, New York, 1908, I, p. 158 (repr. op. p. 164); R. Rey, *Daumier*, 1923, p. 23 (repr.); E. Klossowski, *Honoré Daumier*, Munich, 1923, no. 459, pls. 10-11; A. Alexandre, *Honoré Daumier*, Paris, 1928, p. 32, fig. 51; R. Escholier, *Daumier*, Paris, 1930, p. 128 ff.; H. P. Vincent, *Daumier and His World*, Evanston, 1968.

Edgar Degas (1834-1917)

17. *Portrait of René de Gas*, 1854-55

Pencil on paper, 10¾ x 8⅝ inches

Atelier stamp at lower left

This charming profile of the artist's little brother René, then about age nine, is approached with a sensitivity in keeping with our subject's somnolent condition. The boy has undoubtedly dozed off while posing, closed his eyes, and let his mouth fall open as his sleep deepens. This drawing is among a series of portraits of the artist's brothers and sisters done in the earliest stages of Degas's independent career. At this time, a recognizable style had already formed, influenced by Ingres, Delacroix, and the art of the Renaissance.

This portrait of René owes a good deal to Leonardo and Raphael, whose drawings Degas copied at the Cabinet des Estampes of the Bibliothèque Nationale. Although this is a solidly constructed drawing, its delicacy of line and modeling suggest a tender stillness, a pencil drawn softly across paper in deference to the sleeping child. This is evidence of the nascent psychological penetration which was subsequently developed in the great portraits of his relatives in the Bellelli and Morbilli families painted in Italy between 1858 and 1865.

P.F.B.

PROVENANCE
Atelier Degas; Jean Nepveu-Degas; Wildenstein, New York, 1966.

EXHIBITIONS
Allentown Art Museum, 1977; Pittsburgh, Carnegie Institute, 1979.

Edgar Degas (1834-1917)

18. *Interior (Le Viol)*, 1868-69

Oil on canvas, 32 x 45 inches

Signed at bottom right: *Degas*

The smoldering sensuality and psycho-sexual tension between the man and woman have caused this painting to be known as *Le Viol* (The Rape). Degas referred to it in more neutral terms, as his *Genre Painting*, or simply the *Interior*. Theodore Reff has identified the primary literary source as chapter twenty-one of Emil Zola's *Thérèse Raquin*: "Zola describes the wedding night of Thérèse and her lover Laurent, who have murdered her first husband and waited over a year to avoid arousing suspicion and now begin to discover that their tormented consciences will not only prevent any intimacy, but will eventually drive them to despair and suicide."[1]

Although we know our picture is something other than the aftermath of a rape, the scene is carefully constructed to convey the feelings indicated by Zola. However, instead of indulging in the naturalist writer's naïve presumptions of the possibility of recreating "real life," Degas has taken visual liberties with Zola's text in the creation of a dense and emotionally charged confrontation. Though the basic scene with the flickering fire and the lamp comes from *Thérèse Raquin*, Degas has pushed light and shadow to extraordinary expressive lengths. Thérèse, the light emphasizing her pathetic posture, and Laurent, cast into satanic shadow, are insightful psychological character studies.

The critical convention of Degas's misogyny, established even in the nineteenth century, has been the subject of a thoughtful revaluation by Norma Brouda.[2] Though she does not deal directly with the *Interior*, her remarks on other pictures involving male-female confrontation, of which our painting is a key work among five, argue against misogyny as a motivating factor in selection of this scene as subject matter. Zola's vision of mutual guilt offered the perfect vehicle for the "expressive physiognomy" Degas wished to employ.

P.F.B.

NOTES

[1]T. Reff, *The Artist's Mind*, New York, 1976, p. 205. See pp. 204-213. Reff suggests *Madeleine Férat* as the source of several otherwise inexplicable items in the picture, p. 207.

[2]N. Brouda, "Degas's 'Misogyny,'" *The Art Bulletin*, LIX, Mar., 1977, pp. 95-96.

PROVENANCE

Durand-Ruel; A. A. Pope, Farmington; H. Whittemore, Naugatuck; J. H. Whittemore Co.

EXHIBITIONS

New York, Metropolitan Museum of Art, 1924-26; London, Royal Academy of Arts, 1932, no. 438 (comm. cat.: no. 346, pl. 126); Boston, Museum of Fine Arts, 1935, no. 13 (repr); Paris, Galerie Paul Rosenberg, 1936, no. 17; Philadelphia Museum of Art, 1936, no. 23, (repr.); Cambridge, Mass., Fogg Art Museum, 1936; Paris, Palais National des Arts, 1937, no. 303; Paris, Musée de l'Orangerie, 1937, no. 20, pl XI; New York, Museum of Modern Art, 1944, p. 20 (repr.) 219; Philadelphia Museum of Art, 1947, no. 12; Philadelphia Museum of Art, 1949; San Francisco, The California Palace of the Legion of Honor, 1962; Allentown Art Museum, 1977; Pittsburgh, Carnegie Institute, 1979.

LITERATURE

P.-A. Lemoisne, *Degas*, Paris, n. d. [1912], pp. 61-62, pl. XXIII; P. Jamot, "Degas," *Gazette des Beaux-Arts*, 60, Apr.-Jun., 1918, p. 131 (repr.); J. Meier-Graefe, *Degas*, London, 1923, pp. 28, 30, pl. 32; P. Jamot, *Degas*, Paris, 1924, pp. 70, 72, 84, pl. 41; A. Vollard, *Degas*, Paris, 1924, p. 68 (repr.); G. Rivière, *Degas*, Paris, 1935, pp. 49, 97 (repr.); G. Grappe, *Degas*, Paris, n.d. [1936], p. 51 (repr.); A. Vollard, *Degas*, New York, 1937, pl. 55; P. Pool, *Degas*, London, 1963, pl. 25 (repr. in color); Q. Bell, *Degas: Le Viol* (Charlton Lectures on Art) Newcastle-upon-Tyne, 1965; F. Russoli and F. Minervino, *L'Opera completa di Degas*, Milan, 1970, p. 104, no. 374, pl. XXIII (repr. in color); T. Reff, "Degas's Tableau de Genre," *The Art Bulletin*, LIV, Sept., 1972, pp. 316-337; T. Reff, *The Artist's Mind*, New York, 1976, pp. 200-238 (repr. in color); N. Brouda, "Degas's 'Misogyny,'" *The Art Bulletin*, LIX, Mar., 1977, pp. 95-96; K. Roberts, *Painters of Light, The World of Impressionism*, Oxford, 1978, pp. 24-25 (repr. in color); J.-J. Lévêque, *Edgar Degas*, Paris, 1978, pp. 58-60 (repr.); I. Dunlop, *Degas*, London, 1979, p. 81, pl. 66 (repr. in color); J. Dufwa, *Winds from the East*, Stockholm, 1981, pp. 87-88, fig. 68 (repr.); E. de Keyser, *Degas, Réalité et Métaphore*, Louvain-La-Neuve, 1981, pp. 46, 70-71, 115.

Edgar Degas (1834-1917)

19. *The Ballet Master, Jules Perrot (Le Maitre de Ballet)*, 1875

Essence on gray-green paper, 18⅞ x 11¾ inches

Signed and dated at bottom right: *Degas/1875*

One is at once impressed with the massive solidity of M. Perrot's body and the volume of space which he occupies. This solidity is in part created by the raised viewpoint, showing the relative position of his feet. It is the antithesis of the academic drawings of the time, with the model raised on a dais, and is more akin to the spectator's raised viewpoint found in Japanese prints. This figure reappears in two paintings: *La Classe de Danse*, 1874, in the Louvre and *The Dance Class*, 1876, Bingham Collection in New York. In both of these, he is the pivotal figure around which a dance class takes place. He remains as isolated in the many-figured compositions as he is here, standing with feet apart, solidly occupying his ground, giving direction and purpose to those around him by the slight gesture of his left hand.[1]

Jean Boggs has observed that "Degas, who himself observed the movements of all bodies as critically as Perrot did those of the dancers, saw expressive possibilities in the combination of inertia and sense of authority to be conveyed by Perrot's own body."[2] Degas accomplished all this with the greatest economy of means in the quick drying technique he developed by "soaking the oil out of the colors, diluting them with turpentine . . . and applying them to a matte surface."[3] This allowed him great facility with brush but created an effect that appears at first glance to be chalk. Note the tiny spot of red below the moustache, repeated in a diluted tonality in the shirt front, which gives life to an otherwise somber palette. It is a device he used with great finesse in a number of drawings.

P.F.B.

NOTES

[1] J. S. Boggs, *Drawings by Degas*, St. Louis, 1966, pp. 118-120.
[2] Ibid., p. 118.
[3] T. Reff, *Degas: The Artist's Mind*, New York, 1976, p. 277, no. 25.

EXHIBITIONS

Copenhagen, 1914, no. 703; Paris, Galerie Georges Petit, 1924, no. 54; Northampton, Mass., Smith College Museum of Art, 1933, no. 22; Cambridge, Mass., Fogg Art Museum, 1934, no. 20; Buffalo, Albright Art Gallery, 1935, no. 117 (repr.); Philadelphia Museum of Art, 1936, no. 78 (repr.); Cambridge, Fogg Art Museum, 1936; Boston, Museum of Modern Art, 1938; Cleveland Museum of Art, 1947, no. 67, pl. LIII; Philadelphia Museum of Art, 1947, no. 123; Philadelphia Museum of Art, 1949; Cambridge, Fogg Art Museum, 1958; San Francisco, The California Palace of the Legion of Honor, 1962; St. Louis, etc., 1966 (Philadelphia only); Allentown Art Museum, 1977; Pittsburgh, Carnegie Institute, 1979.

LITERATURE

H. Rivière, *Les dessins de Degas*, Paris, 1922, pl. XXVI; A. Vollard, *Degas*, New York, 1937, pl. 52; E. Degas, *Letters*, Oxford, 1947, repr. op. p. 116, fig. 14; J. Rosenberg, *Great Draughtsmen from Pisanello to Picasso*, Cambridge, 1959, p. 113; L. Browse, *Degas Dancers*, Boston, n. d., p. 343, no. 24 (repr.); J. S. Boggs, *Portraits by Degas*, Berkeley and Los Angeles, 1962, pp. 127-128, repr. pl. 93; J. S. Boggs, *Drawings by Degas*, St. Louis, 1966, pp. 118-120; F. Russoli and F. Minervino, *L'Opera completa di Degas*, Milan, 1970, p. 109, no. 481 (repr.); I. Dunlop, *Degas*, London, 1979, p. 117, pl. 106 (repr.).

Degas
1875

Edgar Degas (1834-1917)

20. *The Foyer of the Dance, Fan (Le Foyer de la Danse)*, ca. 1880

Watercolor, 18 x 20 inches

The pale mauves and blues of this quiet, almost monochromatic watercolor, and the dainty dancers variously disposed—seated, fussing with costumes, or at the bar—make a totally disarming composition. Its bold, geometric division of space is quite unlike Degas's other fans, in which a free play of abstract color forms intersects the dancers in amorphous deep spaces and which use gold and silver, "so that the surfaces themselves would suggest the brilliant artificiality of the theaters in which such fans were meant to be used."[1]

At the 4th Impressionist Exhibition in 1879, Degas and Pissarro exhibited several fans. The Japanese format must have provided a challenge to an inquisitive European sense of the organization of space.

P.F.B.

NOTES

[1]T. Reff, *The Artist's Mind*, New York, 1976, p. 284.

PROVENANCE

M. Exsteens, Paris; E. V. Thaw, New York, 1966.

EXHIBITIONS

Berlin, Galerie Flechteim; Paris, Galerie Charpentier, 1948-49, no. 70; Bern, Kunstmuseum, 1951-52, no. 167; Paris, Gazette des Beaux-Arts, 1955, no. 68; Bern, Kornfeld and Klipstein, Oct.-Nov. 1960, no. 19 (repr.), p. 32; Bern, Kornfeld and Klipstein, 1964 Anniversary Exhibition, no. 11, detail repr. in color; Allentown Art Museum, 1977; Pittsburgh, Carnegie Institute, 1979.

LITERATURE

M. S. Gerstein, "Degas' Fans," *The Art Bulletin*, vol. 64, no. 1, March 1982, pp. 109-110.

Edgar Degas (1834-1917)

21. *Mary Cassatt at the Louvre*, 1880

Pastel on gray paper, 25 x 19¼ inches

Inscribed at upper right: *à mes amis Bartholomé/ degas*

The ambiguous position of the umbrella gives the impression of instability and potential movement of the right arm, and we are given no clues about our subject's context. There is only a masterful abstraction of a woman's back with the arm and its extension, the umbrella, forming a right triangle. The source of this, as Colta Ives has observed,[1] can be found in the single figure Japanese print—the *hashira-e* prints designed to hang on the pillars of houses, or more specifically from Hokusai's *Manga*, "The Strong Woman of Omi Province," as Theodore Reff suggests.[2]

This drawing is titled very specifically, identifying not only Degas's friend and disciple the American painter Mary Cassatt, but also her location. We know this to be true from a fully developed pastel composition and several prints of the same subject. Several points of Miss Cassatt's costume have been touched with color: pink at the neck, red gloves, a strong touch of red at the right hand and pale green on the cuffs. The warm gray highlights on the shoulders and bright touch of red at the right hand are dynamic indicators of the extreme tension to come in her position with her weight shifted to the right where she appears to put an almost impossible burden on the umbrella.

P.F.B.

NOTES

[1]C. F. Ives, *The Great Wave, The Influence of Japanese Woodcuts on French Prints*, New York, 1974, p. 37.

[2]New York, Metropolitan Museum of Art, *Bulletin*, Spring, 1977, Vol. XXXIV, no. 4 (unpaged), no. 76.

PROVENANCE

Paul Bartholomé, Paris; Jacques Seligmann & Co., Paris.

EXHIBITIONS

Paris, Galerie Georges Petit, 1924, no. 117; Paris, Musée de l'Orangerie, 1931, no. 125; Philadelphia Museum of Art, 1936, no. 32 (repr.); Paris, Musée de l'Orangerie, 1937, no. 86, pl. XV; Baltimore Museum of Art, 1941-42, no. 157; Philadelphia Museum of Art, 1947, no. 128; Philadelphia Museum of Art, 1949; San Francisco, The California Palace of the Legion of Honor, 1962; Allentown Art Museum, 1977; Pittsburgh, Carnegie Institute, 1979.

LITERATURE

P. Lafond, *Degas*, Paris, 1918/19, I, p. 128 (repr.); *ibid.*, II, p. 17; A. Vollard, *Degas*, New York, 1937, pl. 13; E. Degas, *Letters* (Eng. ed.), Oxford, 1947, repr. op. p. 152, fig. 18; C. Mauclair, *Degas*, London, n.d., p. 87 (repr.); D. C. Rich, *Degas*, New York, 1953, pl. 38; *Apollo*, 66, Sept., 1957, p. 61 (repr.); P. Pool, *Degas*, London, 1963, pl. 37 (repr. in color); F. Russoli and F. Minervino, *L'Opera completa di Degas*, Milan, 1970, p. 113, no. 577 (repr.); L. H. Giese, "A Visit to the Museum," *Bulletin of the Museum of Fine Arts, Boston*, vol. 76, 1978, pp. 46-47, fig. 7 (repr.); I. Dunlop, *Degas*, London, 1979, pp. 166-167, pl. 159 (repr.).

Degas

Edgar Degas (1834-1917)

22. *Little Dancer of Fourteen Years (Petite Danseuse de Quatorze Ans)*, after the wax executed 1880

Bronze, tulle and silk, 39 inches high

Cast by A.-A. Hébrard in 1921, proof G

The appearance of this piece in the Sixth Impressionist Exhibition in 1881 occasioned the same startled response we have today to works of the sculptor Duane Hanson. The only piece of Degas's sculpture exhibited during his lifetime, the *Dancer* was first shown in the original wax. Dressed in a linen bodice, a gauze tutu, and satin slippers, she had real hair and the costume was finished with a pale green silk bow tied around the braid. It has taken nearly one hundred years for comparably disturbing "super-realist" works to appear.

The Little Dancer met a mixed critical reception in 1881. Sympathetic critics such as Charles Ephrussi, although finding her "frightfully ugly" recognized the modernity of the subject: "This is certainly not the Terpsichore of classic lines, it is the modern 'ballet rat,' learning her trade with her being, all her bad instincts and mean longings. Here is truly a new effort, an attempt at realism in sculpture."[1]

Charles Millard has discussed the figure: "The voids that penetrate the figure—between the legs, between the arms, and between the arms and the torso—provide a continuous flow of space through and around the piece, creating a constant opening and closing effect as the observer walks around it. . . . Degas had, thus, started to break down the traditional hierarchy of views in favor of a continuous three-dimensional experience, and suggestions of planarity . . . have completely disappeared."[2] Degas has removed the frozen statue from its pedestal and made it share the viewer's space. The work is to be perceived by a moving spectator rather than admiring the monumentality of a single view.

Although Degas was not noted as a sculptor during his lifetime and his influence was negligible—*The Little Dancer* was not seen in public again after 1881 until it was cast in bronze after World War I—he was by no means an amateur. Millard insists that "in a more profound sense, Degas's sculpture is a very paradigm of the development of sculpture in 19th century France, a résumé of its statements and problems, its exploratory and conservative strains. . . ."[3] Degas was an indefatigable experimenter in all media, and here proves himself a master of three-dimensional form.

P.F.B.

NOTES

[1]C. E. Ephrussi, "Exposition des artistes indépendants," *La Chronique des arts et de la curiosité*, 16 April 1881, p. 126 (reprinted in Charles W. Millard, *The Sculpture of Degas*, Princeton, 1976, Appendix, pp. 119-120).

[2]Charles W. Millard, *The Sculpture of Degas*, Princeton, 1976, p. 98.

[3]Ibid., p. 47.

PROVENANCE

André Schoeller, Paris.

EXHIBITIONS

Cambridge, Mass., Fogg Art Museum, 1936; Philadelphia Museum of Art, 1936, no. 101; Boston, Museum of Modern Art, 1938; Philadelphia Museum of Art, 1949; Philadelphia Museum of Art, 1950, no. 108; San Francisco, The California Palace of the Legion of Honor, 1962; Allentown Art Museum, 1977; Pittsburgh, Carnegie Institute, 1979.

LITERATURE

J. Rewald, *Degas, Works in Sculpture*, New York, 1944, no. 20; *Art News*, 49, June, 1950, p. 31 (repr.); J. Rewald, *Degas Sculpture*, New York, 1956, pp. 16-20, pl. 24-29, no. XX; J. Canady, *Mainstreams of Modern Art*, New York, 1959, p. 207, 238; T. Reff, *Degas: The Artist's Mind*, New York, 1976, pp. 239-248, reprinted from "Degas Sculpture, 1880-1884," *Art Quarterly*, Vol. XXXIII, Autumn, 1970, pp. 276-298; C. Millard, *The Sculpture of Degas*, Princeton, 1976, pp. 27-34.

Edgar Degas (1834-1917)

23. *Woman Drying Herself (Femme S'Essuyant)*, ca. 1886

Pastel, 21⅝ x 28 inches

Atelier stamp at lower left

An important theme of Degas's work, to which he turned after about ten years of concentration on ballet dancers, was women observed in the intimacy of their bath. These works continue his interest in animal locomotion and often give awkward positions of the model with absolute candor.

As Degas's career progressed, his subjects became more anonymous. The face of this woman drying herself is a hot smudge, with the nose and eyes summarily indicated. Yet the work is completely realized, carefully structured in form through a revolutionary technique of pastel. Instead of blending the chalks for a smooth finish, Degas has superimposed several layers of hatchings. Rather than dissolving the form with these detached strokes, as his Impressionist colleague Monet dissolved form in a riot of light created with short detached strokes, Degas modeled the woman's body into a very convincing volume and even described the surface of her flesh.

The acid tonalities of the shadowy right side, greens over gray-green, move in deliberate progression through orange over yellow with some green to green over orange on the left. The body is modeled with greater density of hatching on a yellow ground with smoky red and greens in shadows.

From about 1875, Degas's eyesight began to fail; he was almost totally blind by 1896. He started using pastel as a primary medium around 1869 in order to take advantage of the possibilities of its greater tonal range. The linear quality of his early work persisted. Although the image begins to soften, the form remains solid.

P.F.B.

PROVENANCE

Atelier Degas (1st sale, no. 132, repr.), Paris; Georges Viau (1st sale, 1942, no. 70, repr.), Paris; Bignou, Paris; Reid and Lefevre, London; James Archdale, Birmingham; Reid and Lefevre, London, 1962.

EXHIBITIONS

London, Lefevre Gallery, 1950, no. 7 (repr.), Bern, Kunstmuseum, 1951-52, no. 43; Edinburgh, Edinburgh Festival, 1952, no. 23, pl. VIII; Birmingham, City of Birmingham Museum and Art Gallery, 1953, no. 125; San Francisco, The California Palace of the Legion of Honor, 1962; Allentown Art Museum, 1977; Pittsburgh, Carnegie Institute, 1979.

LITERATURE

G. Rivière, *M. Degas*, Paris, 1935, p. 113 (repr. in color); P.-A. Lemoisne, *Degas*, Paris, 1946, Vol. III, p. 516, no. 886, p. 517 (repr.); Douglas Cooper, *Pastels by Edgar Degas*, New York, 1953, pp. 13, 24-25, no. 25, (repr. in color).

Pierre-Auguste Renoir (1841-1919)

24. *Mlle. Legrand (La Fillette Attentive)*, 1875

Oil on canvas, 32 x 23½ inches

Signed and dated at bottom right: *Renoir .75*

In 1875 an auction sale of impressionist paintings brought Renoir less than one hundred francs each for ten paintings.[1] It was only through portraits such as this one that he made money from his work. Painted the year after the First Impressionist Exhibition, this is an important painting for Renoir, for Mlle. Legrand was the daughter of an art dealer. The little girl's precious possessions, her earrings, her necklace, and her ring are treated as important extensions of her personality. She is brushed and beribboned, a well-bred child, her hands neatly folded, posture correct, to pose for her portrait. Renoir, perhaps with tongue in cheek, takes a formal approach to a little girl playing grown-up, and the effect of her poise is totally disarming.

The painting's sources can be found in Manet, in the handling of the black dress, and ultimately in the charm of the eighteenth century painters Renoir so admired, Boucher and Fragonard. It is a classically beautiful work of an ideal type of beauty. As a portrait, it is an unqualified success.

P.F.B.

NOTES

[1]J. Rewald, *The History of Impressionism*, New York, 1973, p. 354.

PROVENANCE

Bernheim-Jeune, Paris; Paul Rosenberg, Paris.

EXHIBITIONS

Paris, April, 1876; Paris, Durand-Ruel, 1912; Paris, Bernheim-Jeune Galleries, 1913; Paris, rue de la Ville-l'Evêque, 1923; Paris, Musée de l'Orangerie, 1933, no. 21 (Album, repr. pl. XV); Cambridge, Mass., Fogg Art Museum, 1936; New York, Metropolitan Museum of Art, 1937, no. 11 (repr.); Philadelphia Museum of Art, 1937; New York, Wildenstein Galleries, 1938, no. 35 (repr.); New York, Wildenstein Galleries, 1945, no. 37; Philadelphia Museum of Art, no. 14; Philadelphia Museum of Art, 1949; Art Institute of Chicago, 1955, no. 33 (repr.); San Francisco, The California Palace of the Legion of Honor, 1962; Allentown Art Museum, 1977; Pittsburgh, Carnegie Institute, 1979.

LITERATURE

J. Meier-Graefe, *Renoir*, Leipzig, 1929, p. 73 (repr.); A. C. Barnes and V. de Mazia, *The Art of Renoir*, New York, 1935, pp. 58n, 63n, 64, and 446; *Magazine of Art*, 30, Jul., 1937, p. 421 (repr.); M. Drucker, *Renoir*, Paris, 1944, pl. 32; G. Jedlicka, *Renoir*, Bern, 1947, pl. 15; *Antiques*, 62, Oct., 1952, p. 290 (repr.); R. Cogniat, *Renoir-Enfants*, Paris, 1958, pl. I (in color); F. Daulte, *A. Renoir, Catalogue Raisonné de l'oeuvre peinte*, Lausanne, 1971, I, p. 415; E. Fezzi, *L'Opera Completa di Renoir*, 1869-1883, Milan, 1972, pp. 97-98, no. 184 (repr.).

Pierre-Auguste Renoir (1841-1919)

25. *Les Grands Boulevards*, 1875

Oil on canvas, 20½ x 25 inches

Signed and dated at bottom right: *Renoir .75*

The dissolution of form in light, a blond palette, and instantaneity inform this fully mature impressionist work. Renoir's colleague, Claude Monet, could have been referring to this picture when he stated that he sought to capture "the envelopment, the same light spread over everywhere. . . ."[1] Renoir seldom chose to celebrate the *enveloppe* quite so fully as he does in this picture of a specific instant of urban street life. Even at the time of his greatest dedication to the impressionist experiment, Renoir was preoccupied with the human figure. Even though the pedestrians of *Les Grands Boulevards* are summarily indicated, they retain great substance and are important points of reference in the shallow foreground.

Renoir has chosen the full light of a sunny spring day to depict the bourgeois prosperity of Baron Haussman's Second Empire Boulevard. *Les Grands Boulevards* is painted with an all-over luminescence and uniformity of brush stroke that provide a unity and rhythm. It is this grace, characteristic feathery brush stroke, and indomitably cheerful color that distinguish Renoir's work.

P.F.B.

NOTES

[1]Monet, October 7, 1890, quoted in Linda Nochlin's *Impressionism and Post-Impressionism, 1874-1904, Sources and Documents*, Englewood Cliffs, 1966, p. 34.

PROVENANCE

Count Armand Doria, Paris (sale, 1899, II, no. 208, p. 147); Oscar Schmitz, Dresden.

EXHIBITIONS

Dresden Museum; Basel, Kunsthalle; Zurich, Kunsthaus; Philadelphia Museum of Art, 1947, no. 13; Philadelphia Museum of Art, 1949; San Francisco, The California Palace of the Legion of Honor, 1962; Allentown Art Museum, 1977; Pittsburgh, Carnegie Institute, 1979.

LITERATURE

L. Bénédite, *Französische Kunst*, Leipzig, n.d., pl. 14; P. Fechter, in *Kunst und Künstler*, 1910, pp. 21, 24 (repr.); J. Meier-Graefe, *Auguste Renoir*, Munich, 1911 (repr. op. p. 78); J. Meier-Graefe, *Auguste Renoir*, Paris, 1912 (repr. op. p. 75); K. Scheffler, in *Kunst und Künstler*, 1920-21, p. 186; J. Meier-Graefe, *Renoir*, Leipzig, 1928, p. 91 (repr.); E. Waldmann, in *Documents*, 6/11, 1930, p. 230 (repr. op. p. 316); J. Rewald, *The History of Impressionism*, New York, 1946, p. 310 (repr); M. S. Fox, *Renoir*, New York, 1953, pl. 25 (in color); F. Novotny, *Pelican History of Art: Painting and Sculpture in Europe, 1780-1880*, Baltimore, 1960, p. 171 (repr.); P. H. Feist, *Auguste Renoir*, Leipzig, 1961, no. 19 (repr. in color); E. Fezzi, *L'Opera completa di Renoir*, 1869-1883, Milan, 1972, pp. 97-98, no. 185, pl. 23 (repr. in color).

Renoir. 75.

Pierre-Auguste Renoir (1841-1919)

26. *Dancing Couple (Study for "Le Bal à Bougival")*, 1883

Pen on white paper, $15^{3}/_{16}$ x $7^{5}/_{16}$ inches

Signed at bottom right: *Renoir*; inscribed at bottom: *elle valsait délicieusement abandonnée entre les bras d'un blond aux allures de canotier*

"Around 1883, a sort of break occurred in my work. I had gone to the end of impressionism and I was reaching the conclusion that I didn't know how either to paint, or to draw. In a word, I was at a dead end."[1] This study for the painting *Le Bal à Bougival* (Museum of Fine Arts, Boston) shows a significant retrenchment by Renoir. The linear pattern in the drawing denotes a disciplined effort on Renoir's part to remove himself from the strictly impressionist milieu. *Pleinairisme* and light no longer threaten form but serve to enhance the dreamy quality of the dancing couple. The fact that the young lady's feet no longer seem to touch the ground is not because she is dissolved in light, but because the radiating line pattern of her partner's suit, her costume, and the shadows on the ground contribute to the swirl of the waltz's motion.

The woman is Suzanne Valadon, who often posed for Impressionist painters. The mother of Maurice Utrillo, she later became a painter herself. Positive identification of the man in this drawing has for years been problematic, some identifying him as Paul Lhôte, others as Lestriguez, both friends and models of Renoir. François Daulte identifies him as Lhôte,[2] author of the short story *Mademoiselle Zélie*, which is the source of the inscription at the bottom of the drawing: "She waltzed beautifully, abandoned in the arms of a blond with the look of a boater."

P.F.B.

NOTES

[1]A. Vollard, *Renoir*, Paris, 1920, p. 135, quoted in J. Rewald, *The History of Impressionism*, 4th ed., New York, 1973, p. 486.
[2]F. Daulte, *A. Renoir, Catalogue Raisonné de l'oeuvre peint*, Lausanne, 1971, I, p. 438.

PROVENANCE

M. Pridnoff, Paris; César de Hauke, Paris.

EXHIBITIONS

Cambridge, Mass., Fogg Art Museum, 1934, no. 62; Buffalo, Albright Art Gallery, 1935, no. 121 (repr.); Philadelphia Museum of Art, 1947, no. 130; Philadelphia Museum of Art, 1950-51, no. 104 (repr.); Cambridge, Fogg Art Museum, 1958; San Francisco, The California Palace of the Legion of Honor, 1962; Allentown Art Museum, 1977; Pittsburgh, Carnegie Institute, 1979.

LITERATURE

La Vie Moderne, Nov. 3, 1883 (repr.); J. Rewald, *Renoir Drawings*, New York, 1946, no. 17 (repr.); R. Bernier, "Le musée privé d'un conservateur," *L'Oeil*, 27, Mar., 1957, p. 22 (repr.); B. Holme, *Master Drawings in Line*, New York, 1958, pl. LX

elle valsait délicieusement abandonnée
entre les bras d'un blond aux allures
de canotier.

Camille Pissarro (1830-1903)

27. *Baskets*, ca. 1889

Charcoal on paper, 8⅞ x 12 inches

Estate stamp at bottom left: *CP*

The direct simplicity and sincerity with which Pissarro treated landscape and peasant subjects are seen in this study for *The Gleaners*, 1889 (Kunstmuseum, Basel). John Rewald writes that drawing for Pissarro "was not merely an exercise to gain skill or dexterity; it was his way of appropriating what he observed and of communicating intensely with the world around him."[1] This basket is observed five times, as if Pissarro wished to know it from all angles, to understand its volume, and to tell us of its simple grandeur. There is nothing flamboyant or showy in his method, and nothing which is non-essential to the message.

P.F.B.

NOTES

[1]J. Rewald, *Camille Pissarro*, New York, n.d. [1963], p. 49.

PROVENANCE

Ludovic-Rodo Pissarro, Paris; John Rewald (sale, Sotheby's, Jul. 7, 1960, no. 92 repr.).

EXHIBITIONS

East Hampton, New York, Guild Hall, 1952, no. 42; Los Angeles Municipal Art Gallery, 1959, no. 102; San Francisco, The California Palace of the Legion of Honor, 1962; Allentown Art Museum, 1977; Pittsburgh, Carnegie Institute, 1979.

LITERATURE

J. Rewald, *Pissarro*, Paris, 1948, no. 7 (repr.); J. Rewald, *Pissarro*, New York, 1954, pl. 37; J. Rewald, *Camille Pissarro*, New York, n.d. [1963], p. 49; *Pissarro*, exhibition catalogue, Hayward Gallery, London, 1981, p. 130.

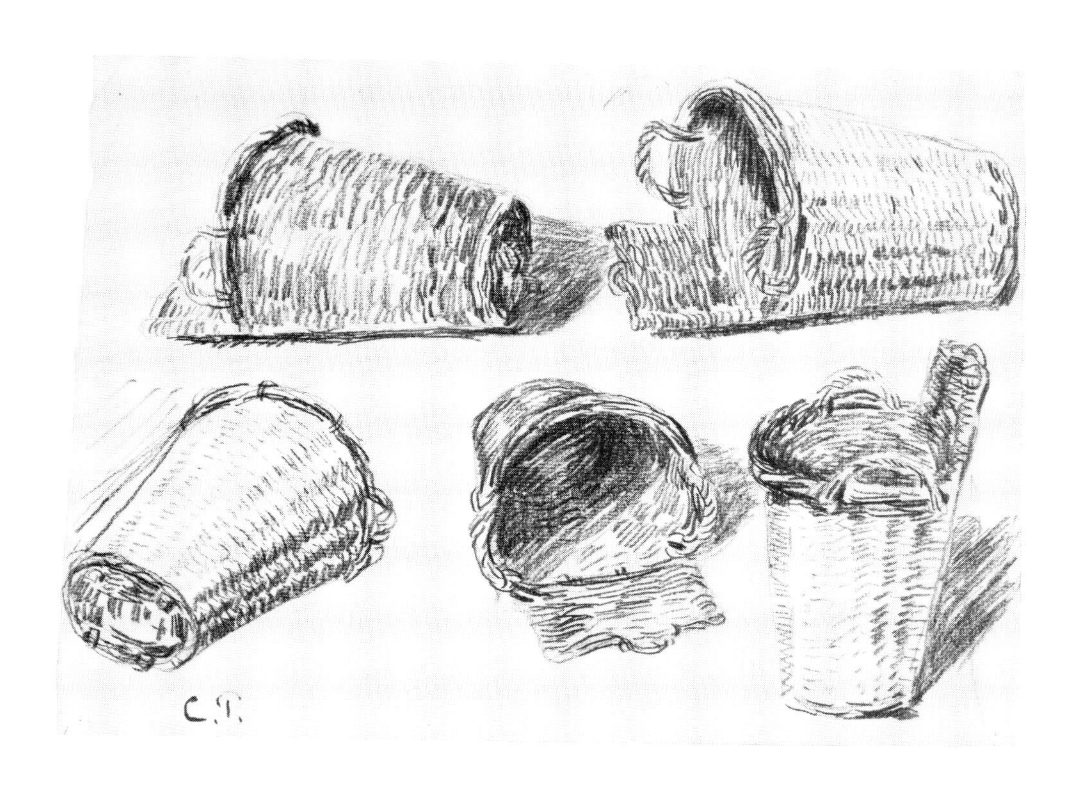
C.P.

Paul Cézanne (1839-1906)

28. *Mme. Cézanne (Mme. Cézanne au corsage rayé)*, ca. 1883-87

Oil on canvas, 24½ x 20⅛ inches

Schapiro, who suggested the kinship of this image with a traditional *mater dolorosa*, wrote: "In the light key, with the almost shadowless face against a light ground, in the exquisite relation of the warm and cool tints of the face to the grayer wall, the painting is Impressionist in spirit. In the Impressionist portraits the inner life of the woman is often overlooked for the sake of an outward charm which requires an open smiling face and features like blossoms. In retaining from this art the softness of the features and the beauty of the skin, Cézanne has produced a tender image of ascetic feeling."[1]

The almost perfect oval of the face is carefully counterbalanced by the opposite thrust of the shadow of the jaw and the ear. The whole is further brought into equilibrium by the curious gray spot over the head. It is hardly the shadow of a corner, for it stops without reason when its function in bringing the movement of the picture to a precarious balance is achieved. The cap of the sleeve on the left serves a similar function, for we find no such structure on the sleeve on the right.

P.F.B.

NOTES

[1]M. Schapiro, *Paul Cézanne*, New York, 1952, p. 58, ill. p. 57.

PROVENANCE

Ambroise Vollard, Paris; Halvorsen, Oslo; Dr. G. F. Reber, Munich; Paul Rosenberg, Paris; Samuel Courtauld, London; Paul Rosenberg, Paris.

EXHIBITIONS

Paris, Salon d'Automne, 1904, no. 3; Rhode Island School of Design, 1930; Paris, Durand-Ruel, 1932, no. 5; Cambridge, Mass., Fogg Art Museum, 1934; Chicago, 1934, no. 297; Philadelphia Museum of Art, 1934, no. 13; Paris, Musée de l'Orangerie, 1936, no. 58; Philadelphia Museum of Art, 1937; Boston, Museum of Fine Arts, Institute of Modern Art, 1939, no. 13 (repr.); Cambridge, Fogg Art Museum, 1941; Philadelphia Museum of Art, 1947, no. 21; Philadelphia Museum of Art, 1949; San Francisco, The California Palace of the Legion of Honor, 1962; Allentown Art Museum, 1977; Pittsburgh, Carnegie Institute, 1979; Philadelphia Museum of Art, 1983, no. 15.

LITERATURE

A. Vollard, *Paul Cézanne*, Paris, 1914, pl. 46; E. Faure, in *L'Amour de l'Art*, I, 1920, p. 267 (repr.); A. Zeisho, *Paul Cézanne*, 1921, pl. 2; J. Meier-Graefe, *Cézanne und sein Kreis*, Munich, 1922, p. 129 (repr.); G. Rivière, *Le Maître Paul Cézanne*, Paris, 1923, p. 201; K. Pfister, *Cézanne, Gestalt-Werk-Mythos*, Potsdam, 1927, pl. 72; J. Meier-Graefe, *Cézanne*, New York, 1927, pl. 49; *L'Amour de l'Art*, I, 1929, p. 17 (repr.); M. Damery, in *L'Amour de l'Art*, 10, Jan. 1929, p. 17 (repr.); *Parnassus*, 2, May, 1930, p. 25 (repr.); L. Venturi, *Cézanne, son art–son oeuvre*, Paris, 1936, I, no. 527; ibid., II, pl. 163 (b. rt.); A. Barnes and V. de Mazia, *The Art of Cézanne*, New York, 1939, pp. 14n, 313n, 343, 412 (no. 98); B. Dorival, *Cézanne*, Paris, 1948, pl. III; M. Schapiro, *Cézanne*, New York, 1952, p. 58 (repr. in color); T. Rousseau, *Paul Cézanne*, New York, 1953, pl. 14 (in color); F. Novotny (intro.), *Cézanne*, New York, Phaidon, n.d., no. 48 (repr.).

Paul Cézanne (1839-1906)

29. *View of Mont Sainte-Victoire*, ca. 1885-90

Watercolor, 15¼ x 19⅞ inches

Lent by Fogg Art Museum, Harvard University, Cambridge, Massachusetts, Gift of Henry P. McIlhenny.

It is in his late watercolors that Cézanne came closest to pure abstraction. The transparent medium allowed him a lyrical delicacy of color and touch impossible with oil. In this small work done between 1885 and 1890, we see a step in the direction of the gentle poetry of the watercolors to come. The contour of the mountain is clearly defined and we know exactly where we are in the landscape. It is difficult to assign a specific role to the marks within the boundaries of the mountain and it is only by geometric and color indications that we can distinguish houses and trees. By means of this evenness of description Cézanne has brought the entire landscape into plane, treating the slopes and crags of his mountain with equal detail as the foreground trees and houses. The surface of the paper is not denied; neither is the looming bulk of the mountain. This little painting triumphs in reconciling the majesty of nature with the abstract genius of Cézanne's art.

P.F.B.

PROVENANCE

Vicomte d'Hendcourt, London (sale, Sotheby's, 1929, no. 165, repr.); P. Rosenberg; Paul J. Sachs; Jacques Seligmann & Co., New York; gift to Harvard, 1957.

EXHIBITIONS

London, Burlington Fine Arts Club, 1922, no. 67; New York, Museum of Modern Art, 1929, no. 30 (repr.); Northampton, Mass., Smith College Museum of Art, 1933; New York, Jacques Seligmann Galleries, 1933, no. 16; Philadelphia Museum of Art, 1934, no. 56; Buffalo, Albright Art Gallery, 1935, no. 125 (repr.); San Francisco Museum of Art, 1937, no. 44 (repr.); New York, Marie Harriman Gallery, 1939, no. 23; Boston, Museum of Fine Arts, 1945, p. 3; Philadelphia Museum of Art, 1947; Philadelphia Museum of Art, 1949; Cambridge, Mass., Fogg Art Museum, 1958; San Francisco, The California Palace of the Legion of Honor, 1962; Washington, D.C., The Phillips Collection, 1971, no. 43; Allentown Art Museum, 1977; Pittsburgh, Carnegie Institute, 1979; Philadelphia Museum of Art, 1983, no. 28.

LITERATURE

Burlington Magazine, 40, June, 1922, p. 267 (repr.); L. Venturi, *Cézanne, son art–son oeuvre*, Paris, 1936, I, no. 1561; ibid., II (repr.); J. Canaday, *Mainstreams of Modern Art*, New York, 1959, p. 356, fig. 432; J. Rewald, *Paul Cézanne, The Watercolors, A Catalogue Raisonné*, Boston, to be published 1984, no. 200.

Paul Cézanne (1839-1906)

30. *Peasant Girl Wearing a Fichu (Jeune Paysanne)*, 1890-93

Graphite on white laid paper, watermark Michallet, 6⅛ x 8⅝ inches

Despite the careful structuring of volume created with a series of short parallel strokes, Cézanne presents a beautiful young girl with a freshness that belies the careful procedure. We detect a shyness and naïveté, but the strokes of the pencil on paper betray nothing hesitant or unsure. The model remains unidentified, which is unfortunate since Cézanne rarely treated with such intimacy a portrait subject beyond his family circle.

Chappuis assigns the date of 1873 to this drawing, but we must agree with his reviewers, Kenneth Clark and Theodore Reff, that it more properly belongs to a later period.[1]

P.F.B.

NOTES

[1]A. Chappuis, *The Drawings of Paul Cézanne, A Catalogue Raisonné*, Greenwich, Conn., 1973, I, no. 273, p. 108; K. Clark, "The Enigma of Cézanne," *Apollo*, XCX, no. 149, July 1974, pp. 79-80, review of Chappuis's *Catalogue* places drawing at "end of Cézanne's Classic period" and suggests possible date of 1893 for both drawing and etching referred to by Vollard in connection with Venturi no. 1160 and states, "there is no certainty that they are related to each other . . ."; T. Reff, *The Burlington Magazine*, CXVII, July, 1975, pp. 489-491, questions Chappuis's date and disassociates the drawing and etching referred to by Vollard.

PROVENANCE

Doctor Gachet; Paul Gachet, Auvers-sur-Oise; Galerie Daber, Paris, 1962.

EXHIBITIONS

Paris, Musée de l'Orangerie, 1936, no. 145; Allentown Art Museum, 1977; Pittsburgh, Carnegie Institute, 1979; Philadelphia Museum of Art, 1983, no. 30.

LITERATURE

L. Venturi, *Cézanne, son art–son oeuvre*, Paris, 1936, I, p. 347; J. Rewald, *Cézanne et Zola*, Paris, 1936, p. 81; P. Gachet, *Cézanne à Auvers, Cézanne Graveur*, Paris, 1952 (mentioned with Venturi no. 1160); A. Chappuis, *The Drawings of Paul Cézanne, A Catalogue Raisonné*, Greenwich, Conn., 1973, I, no. 273, p. 108; K. Clark, "The Enigma of Cézanne," *Apollo*, XCX, no. 149, July, 1974, pp. 79-80; T. Reff, *The Burlington Magazine*, CXVII, July, 1975, pp. 489-491.

Vincent Van Gogh (1853-1890)

31. *Road at Saintes-Maries*, 1888

Reed pen and brown ink, 11½ x 19¼ inches

Van Gogh's visit to the fishing village of Sts.-Maries, near Arles, in 1888, was a joyous one, recorded by a number of paintings and drawings. Among these are four drawings of the cottages lining the village street. Van Gogh experimented freely with reed pens in these drawings, producing a great variety of textures with line pattern and stipple.

This drawing is the most conventional of the four and exhibits Van Gogh's splendid gifts as a vigorous traditional draughtsman. We are situated at a relatively low point of view, and presented with an infinite space receding along the road that goes past the cottage doors. It is a homely drawing that recalls his Dutch compatriot Rembrandt, who recorded similar scenes in the Netherlands with pen and bistre ink. Although *Road at Saintes-Maries* appears in Van Gogh's oeuvre among some of the most freely experimental of his drawings, it reflects his clearly acknowledged debt to the artists whom he considered his masters. While we may see shades of Rembrandt here in the subject, the robust vocabulary of marks is purely Van Gogh's.

P.F.B.

PROVENANCE

Mrs. S. Van Gogh-Bonger; Paul Cassirer Art Gallery, Berlin; H. Simon, Frankfurt; Wildenstein Gallery, New York; F. H. Hirschland, Harrison, New York; Mr. and Mrs. H. Hirschland, Berkeley Heights; H. Berggruen, Paris; R. M. Light & Co., Boston, 1975.

EXHIBITIONS

Amsterdam, Municipal Museum, 1905, no. 379; Berlin, 1927-28, no. 103; New York, etc. 1935-36, no. 111; New York, 1943, no. 2 and 73; San Francisco, 1947, no. 131; Cleveland, 1948, no. 43; New York, 1955, no. 2 and no. 99; Allentown Art Museum, 1977; Pittsburgh, Carnegie Institute, 1979.

LITERATURE

J.-B. de la Faille, *The Works of Vincent Van Gogh*, Amsterdam, 1970, p. 504, F. 1436; *Letters*, nos. 499 and 500 (probably June 22, 1888); J. Hulsker, *The Complete Van Gogh*, Amsterdam, 1977, New York, 1980, p. 332, no. 1454 (repr.).

Vincent Van Gogh (1853-1890)

32. *Rain*, 1889

Oil on canvas, 28⅞ x 36⅜ inches

Van Gogh did numerous paintings of the enclosed wheat field outside the window of his workroom at the Asylum St. Paul de Mausolée at St. Rémy, works which explore the expressive possibilities of different times of day and seasons. The elements of the landscape remained constant: a diagonal ditch in the foreground, walls at the left and back of the field, and the hills in the background. These are disturbing pictures, for the lines of the tilled field converging on a conventional one-point perspective are abruptly stopped by the wall, and there is only the vaguest indication of a middle ground beyond the wall. In *Rain*, the viewer is forced to remain at the plane of the surface of the canvas not only because of the high viewpoint but because of the confounding and irregular pattern of falling rain superimposed upon the pattern of the field. The overall tonalities of the picture are now darker and warmer due to gradual color change in the exposed areas of the canvas, but the pale blues and olives are typical of the colors he used at St. Rémy.

Van Gogh mentions this painting in a letter of 26 October 1889: "I have a rain effect going." The rapid strokes are applied over a high impasto which has had sufficient time to dry to remain undisturbed by the diagonal slashes. Between 1886 and 1888 in Paris, Van Gogh was impressed by the Japanese print *Sudden Shower at Ohashi* by Hiroshige and made a copy of it. While the influence here is unmistakable, it has been internalized and given back as a thoroughly bold invention.

P.F.B.

PROVENANCE

Mme. H. von Tschudi, Munich; Paul Rosenberg, New York, 1950.

EXHIBITIONS

Amsterdam, Municipal Museum, 1905, no. 209a; Munich, Neue Staatsgalerie; Paris, 1932, no. 55; Brussels, 1935, no. 102; New York, Museum of Modern Art, 1935, no. 52 (repr.); Paris, Exposition Internationale, 1937; Belgrade, 1939, no. 61; Buenos Aires, etc., 1939-40, no. 70; Philadelphia Museum of Art, 1949; Philadelphia Museum of Art, 1950, no. 99; San Francisco, The California Palace of the Legion of Honor, 1962; New York, Guggenheim Museum, 1964; Allentown Art Museum, 1977; Pittsburgh, Carnegie Institute, 1979; Washington, D.C., National Gallery of Art, 1980.

LITERATURE

L. Piérard, *La vie tragique de Vincent Van Gogh*, Paris, 1924, pl. 44; J.-B. de la Faille, *L'oeuvre de Vincent Van Gogh*, Paris, 1928, I, no. 650; *ibid.*, II, pl. CLXXXII; F. Fels, *Vincent Van Gogh*, Paris, 1928, p. 137 (repr.); V. Van Gogh, *Further Letters to His Brother*, London, 1929, letter 613, p. 407; M. Florisoone, *Van Gogh*, Paris, 1937, p. 53; Scherjon and de Gruyter, 1937, St. Rémy, no. 65: Letters 613 and 621; J. Rewald, *Post-Impressionism*, New York, 1962, p. 357 (repr.); J.-B. de la Faille, *The Works of Vincent Van Gogh*, Amsterdam, 1970, p. 258, no. 650 [H656]; J. Hulsker, *The Complete Van Gogh*, Amsterdam, 1977, New York, 1980, pp. 424-25, no. 1839 (repr.).

Georges Seurat (1859-1891)

33. *The Trombone Player: Study for "La Parade,"* 1877-88

Conté crayon with gouache on paper, 12½ x 9½ inches

Seurat's scientific formula of color as applied in his large finished compositions creates a somewhat frigid effect. In drawings such as this one, he solved with greater intimacy—if not spontaneity—the problems of tonal range and quality of light. In this case, one of a series studying color in various conditions of light, the artist is out of doors at night. The light source is the gas jets at the top of the drawing. Within the strict geometry of spatial division, we have the silhouetted figure in the right foreground upon whom no light is cast. He remains a spectator, outside the central drama. The trombone player has come to the front, his face, his trombone, and his shirt-front glowing dimly in the reflected light from the audience. The two musicians to the left rear receive the full benefit of a direct light source. All of these conditions are to be found in the final version, *La Parade*, at The Metropolitan Museum of Art, although the strange atmospheric perspective of the shallow space has been flattened.

Teodor de Wyewa, in an article on Seurat's achievement, comments that "there is . . . one field in which it seems to me that Seurat has brought to the fore all the qualities of his genius: I have seen drawings by him, marvelously artistic, sober, luminous, alive, the most expressive drawings I know of."[1] Indeed, the simplicity of means employed here have solved the problem of this particular condition of light, without the ossifying effect of pointillism.

P.F.B.

NOTES

[1]J. Rewald, *Post-Impressionism from Van Gogh to Gauguin*, New York, 2nd ed., 1962, pp. 427-28.

PROVENANCE

G. Jacquart, Paris; Jacques Seligmann & Co., New York.

EXHIBITIONS

Boston, Ritz-Carlton Hotel, 1931; Providence, Rhode Island School of Design, 1931; Cambridge, Mass., Fogg Art Museum, 1934, no. 65; Cambridge, Fogg Art Museum, 1936; New York, Museum of Modern Art, 1944, p. 97; San Francisco, The California Palace of the Legion of Honor, 1947, no. 149 (repr.); Philadelphia Museum of Art, 1947, no. 133; Philadelphia Museum of Art, 1949; New York, Wildenstein Galleries, 1953, no. 34 (repr.); Paris, Musée de l'Orangerie, 1955, no. 92, pl. 93; New York, Museum of Modern Art (etc.), 1958, no. 135; Cambridge, Fogg Art Museum, 1958; San Francisco, The California Palace of the Legion of Honor, 1962; Allentown Art Museum, 1977; Pittsburgh, Carnegie Institute, 1979.

LITERATURE

G. Kahn, *Les Dessins de Georges Seurat*, Paris, 1928, II, pl. 123; R. A. Parker, "The Drawings of Georges Seurat," *International Studio*, 91, Sept., 1928, p. 23; R. J. Goldwater, "Some Aspects of the Development of Seurat's Style," *Art Bulletin*, Jun., 1941, pp. 117-30, fig. 14; J. Rewald, *Georges Seurat*, New York, 1943, no. 75 (repr.), p. 102; *G. Seurat Tegninger*, Copenhagen, pl. 24; G. Seligman, *The Drawings of Georges Seurat*, New York, 1947, p. 60, no. 24; J. Rewald, *Post-Impressionism*, New York, 1962, p. 430 (repr.); H. Dorra and J. Rewald, *Seurat*, Paris, 1959, no. 180b (repr.); C. M. de Hauke, *Seurat et son Oeuvre*, Paris, 1961, II, pp. 260-61, no. 680 (repr.).

Henri de Toulouse-Lautrec (1864-1901)

34. *Portrait of Gustav-Lucien Dennery*, 1883

Charcoal, 24¼ x 18½ inches

Signed at lower left: *T-Lautrec*

Inscribed at lower left, not in artist's hand: *November 1883*; on the verso, a study of a nude

The *Portrait of Gustav-Lucien Dennery* is among the first independent drawings of Toulouse-Lautrec's maturity. It is influenced by the lessons of the academy, where he labored manfully with the artificial impositions upon the naturally exuberant linear style of his youth. These early drawings of his family and friends are intimate portraits and show an informality impossible in the atmosphere of the atelier.

Dennery was a fellow student of Lautrec's in Paris who later achieved some note as a painter in his own right. His pose is architecturally structured with a series of interlocking angles, but the most expressive parts of the model, the head and hand, receive a more fully modeled treatment. We even detect a note of amused cynicism in his face, not out of keeping with the smart accessories of his costume, the derby hat and walking stick of the fashionable young Parisian of the 1880s.

P.F.B.

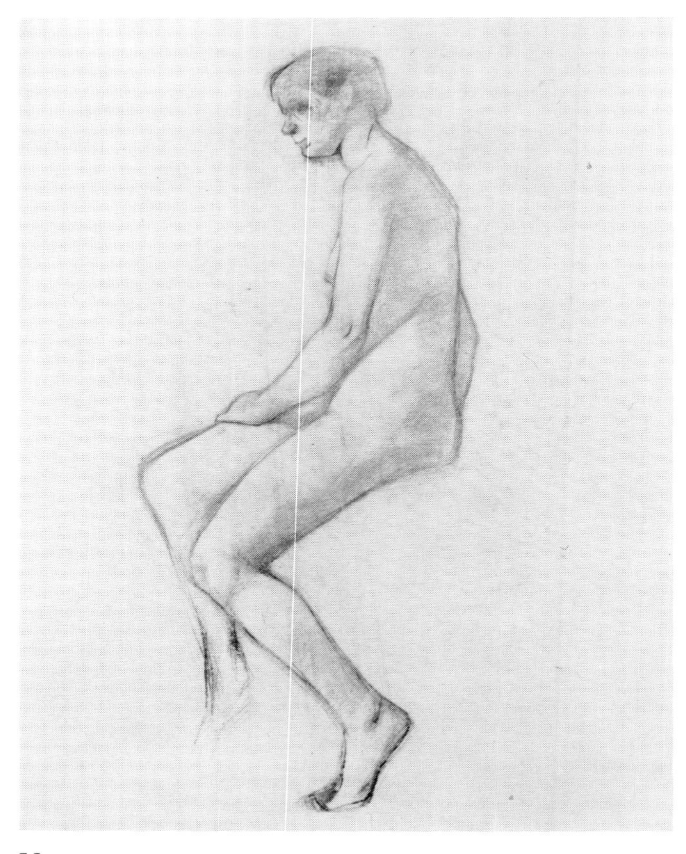

Verso

PROVENANCE

G. Tapié de Céleyran; Mme. W. Feilchenfeldt; R. M. Light, Boston; Mr. and Mrs. John Goelet.

EXHIBITIONS

New York, Charles E. Slatkin Galleries, 1964; Cambridge, Mass., Fogg Art Museum, 1965; Allentown Art Museum, 1977; Pittsburgh, Carnegie Institute, 1979.

LITERATURE

P. A. Wick, *Henri de Toulouse-Lautrec, 1864-1901, Portraits and Figure Studies: The Early Years; an exhibition commemorating the one hundredth anniversary of his birth*, New York, 1964; M. G. Dortu, *Toulouse-Lautrec et son oeuvre*, 1971, Vol. V, p. 488, D.2.746 and D.2.747.

Henri de Toulouse-Lautrec (1864-1901)

35. *At the Moulin Rouge: The Dance (La Danse au Moulin Rouge)*, 1890

Oil on canvas, 45½ x 59 inches

Signed and dated top right: *HTLautrec 90*

Of Toulouse-Lautrec's three large many-figured compositions, *La Danse au Moulin Rouge* is considered the most successful. It is also the most subtle in its inner architecture. A diagonal line from the front of the scene to the middle distance was a favorite device adopted by the Impressionists from Japanese prints; Toulouse-Lautrec used it to great effect in many pictures. What appears to be a more classically oriented vertical and horizontal structure here, including a radiating one-point perspective of the floor boards, is actually a similar diagonal progression through the three planes of the painting's space. The hot pink worn by the woman in the foreground is concentrated as red in the dancer's stockings at the center of the composition. From here, her kick leads us to the red-haired page in the upper left, wearing the most concentrated spot of red in the picture. In defiance of the sedate vertical of the dignified lady in pink and the horizontal frieze of people, Lautrec has brought us through the scene in a diagonal thrust, but instead of using a line, he has accomplished it with color.

The Moulin Rouge, through its appearance in many of Toulouse-Lautrec's paintings, has become legend, though he gives few clues in any of these pictures of its exact physical appearance. It is the people of the Paris *demimonde* who held his interest: the female dancer, La Goulue, her topknot falling from its proper place atop her head in the violent dance; Valentin Le Désossé ("The Boneless One"), her partner in the top hat; Jane Avril, the woman inconspicuously placed to Valentin's right, another favorite subject. The group of four men in the center background at the waiter's right are the artist's friends Varney, Guibert, Sescau, and Gauzi.

Lautrec has recorded this scene seemingly without moral comment. If we compare it with the drama and bright freshness of the posters for the Moulin Rouge, however, we sense a more somber meaning. The spectators are unmoved, and only half interested in the dance; each is isolated by his expression. These murky psychological undertones mark this painting as a precursor of the expressionist movement in Norway, Belgium, and Germany.

P.F.B.

PROVENANCE

Sévadjian (sale, 1920, no. 17); Oller; Paul Rosenberg; Arnold Seligmann, Paris.

EXHIBITIONS

Paris, Exposition Permanente au Moulin Rouge de M. Zidler, 1890-93; Paris, Galerie Paul Rosenberg, 1914, no. 29; Paris, Manzi-Joyant, 1914, no. 38; Paris, Musée des Arts Décoratifs, 1925; Paris, Musée des Arts Décoratifs, Pavillon de Marsan, 1931, no. 60; London, M. Knoedler & Co., 1934, no. 1; Boston, Museum of Fine Arts, 1935, no. 50; Cambridge, Mass., Fogg Art Museum, 1936; Philadelphia Museum of Art, 1937; New York, Museum of Modern Art, 1939, no. 79 (repr.); Philadelphia Museum of Art, 1947, no. 34; Philadelphia Museum of Art, 1949; Philadelphia Museum of Art, 1950-51, no. 93 (repr.); Philadelphia Museum of Art, 1955, no. 29 (repr. in color); San Francisco, The California Palace of the Legion of Honor, 1962; Allentown Art Museum, 1977; Pittsburgh, Carnegie Institute, 1979; Washington, D.C., National Gallery of Art, 1980.

LITERATURE

M. Joyant, *Henri de Toulouse-Lautrec*, Paris, 1926, p. 268 (repr. p. 126); *Art Digest*, II, Apr. 1, 1937, p. 8 (repr.); G. Mack, *Toulouse-Lautrec*, New York, 1938, pp. 131, 152, 259, 270; J. Lassaigne, *Toulouse-Lautrec*, Paris, 1939, p. 75 (repr.); G. Jedlicka, *Henri de Toulouse-Lautrec*, Zurich, 1943 (repr. op. p. 172); F. Kimball and L. Venturi, *Great Paintings in America*, New York, 1948, no. 97 (repr. in color); *Art Digest*, 23, Jul. 1, 1949, p. 7 (repr.); Edouard-Joseph, *Dictionnaire biographique des artistes contemporains*, Paris, Librairie Grund, III, p. 245; *Art News*, 50, June, 1951, p. 20 (repr. in color); *The Taste of Our Time: Lautrec*, Geneva, Skira, 1953, pp. 44-45 (repr. in color); H. Tietze, *Toulouse-Lautrec*, New York, n.d. [c. 1953], p. 49 (repr. in color); *Arts*, 30, Nov., 1955, pp. 26-31 (repr. in color); D. Cooper, *Henri de Toulouse-Lautrec*, New York, 1956, p. 88 (repr. in color); P. Courthion, *Montmartre*, Lausanne, 1956, p. 62 (det. repr. in color); R. Bernier, "Le musée privé d'un conservateur," *L'Oeil*, 27, Mar., 1957, p. 23 (repr.); *Art News Annual*, 1959, p. 168 (repr. in color); M. G. Dortu, *Toulouse-Lautrec et son oeuvre*, New York, 1971, Vol. II, p. 190, P. 361, repr. p. 191; R. Thompson, *Toulouse-Lautrec*, London, 1977, p. 50, fig. 22 (repr.); C. F. Stuckey, *Toulouse-Lautrec: Paintings*, Chicago, 1979, pp. 21-22 (repr.); D. Cooper, *Henri de Toulouse-Lautrec*, New York, 1982, p. 78 (repr.); E. Lucie-Smith, *Toulouse-Lautrec*, Oxford, 1983, no. 23 (repr.); F. Novotny, *Toulouse-Lautrec*, New York, 1983, pp. 188-189 (repr.); D. Cooper, *Toulouse-Lautrec, 25 Masterworks*, New York, 1983, p. 20 (repr. in color).

Henri de Toulouse-Lautrec (1864-1901)
36. *Self Portrait*, 1896

Blue crayon on paper, 8⅜ x 7 inches
Monogrammed in red at bottom left

Rapid execution contributes to this self-portrait's quality of caricature. This sketch for the menu "The Crocodile" (D. 200) is among a number of self-portrait sketches that have a comic air. This small drawing in blue reveals an essential component of Lautrec's more fully developed work: his gift as a draughtsman to present in significant gesture the most expressive attitude of his subject.

P.F.B.

PROVENANCE
Pierrefort and J. Cailac, Paris.

EXHIBITIONS
Paris, Musée des Arts Décoratifs, 1931, no. 292; Paris, Musée des Arts Décoratifs, 1931; Philadelphia Museum of Art, 1947, no. 149; Philadelphia Museum of Art, 1955, no. 102; Art Institute of Chicago, no. 102; San Francisco, The California Palace of the Legion of Honor, 1962; Montreal Museum of Fine Arts, 1968, no. 15; Allentown Art Museum, 1977; Pittsburgh, Carnegie Institute, 1979.

LITERATURE
M. Joyant, *Henri de Toulouse-Lautrec*, Paris, 1927, II, p. 247; *Dessins des Maîtres Français*, Fascicule IX (repr.), no. 3; M. Joyant, *70 Dessins de H. de Toulouse-Lautrec*, Paris, 1930 (repr.), no. 3; M. G. Dortu, *Toulouse-Lautrec et son oeuvre*, New York, 1971, Vol. V, D.4.229.

Edouard Vuillard (1868-1940)

37. *The Meal (Le Petit Déjeuner)*, ca. 1899

Oil on cardboard, 18½ x 18¾ inches

Signed at top right: *E. Vuillard*

Lent by the Philadelphia Museum of Art, gift of Henry P. McIlhenny, retaining life interest.

"A picture—before being a horse, a nude, or an anecdote—is essentially a flat surface covered with colors assembled in a certain order." This famous statement by Maurice Denis, Vuillard's colleague in the Nabis group of painters, sums up their rejection of naturalism in favor of the poetic value of the decorative qualities of painting. *The Meal* aptly illustrates this concept, yet Vuillard's individuality is not overshadowed, and it is the intimate quality that here overcomes any aesthetic theory.

Coloristically and spatially, *The Meal* seems to have evolved from a Coromandel screen, with geometric planes providing the background for linear human figures. Japanese prints, with their decorative spatial arrangements and flat areas of color, are acknowledged to have had a major influence in the Nabis group.[1] The harmonious displacement of colors here seems to suggest this influence, yet the hot pink rose behind the baby's head, the only discordant note in the painting, not only draws attention to the baby, but attests to Vuillard's strong personality as a painter. There is no harshness of the overall effect in spite of the clearly delineated contours; rather, light seems to have been filtered through curtains.

Balance is achieved by placing the small child with her light colored clothes and chair against the darker background, and the grandmother, a much bulkier figure, against the soft gray plane. The foreground objects seem out of focus. Vuillard consistently chose subjects from his immediate family: in *The Meal* the artist's mother is feeding his sister's daughter, Annette Rousel. One can almost follow the little girl's development through Vuillard's paintings.

A.D.F.

NOTES

[1]G. Needham, *Japonisme: Japanese Influence on French Art 1854-1910*, Cleveland, 1975, pp. 125-26.

PROVENANCE

Paul Rosenberg, Paris, 1938.

EXHIBITIONS

Philadelphia Museum of Art, 1947, no. 101; Philadelphia Museum of Art, 1949; New York, Museum of Modern Art, 1954, p. 73 (repr.), 102; San Francisco, The California Palace of the Legion of Honor, 1962; Allentown Art Museum, 1977; Pittsburgh, Carnegie Institute, 1979.

LITERATURE

Life, 37, Nov. 1, 1954, pp. 74-78 (repr. in color); S. Preston, *Edouard Vuillard*, New York, n.d. [1974], p. 30, repr. fig. 36.

E Vuillard

Henri Matisse (1869-1954)

38. *Study for "The White Plumes,"* 1919

Pencil on white paper, 20⅝ x 14 inches

Signed at the bottom right: *Henri Matisse 1919*

This study is among a series of drawings that, according to Alfred Barr, "expresses a range of mood and characterization quite extraordinary for Matisse, who portrays the model almost as if she were an actress or mime assuming a variety of roles."[1] Barr also records Margaret Scolari's recollection of the remarkable hat, which Matisse made himself: "He bought the straw foundation and the feathers and the black ribbon and put it together with pins on the model's head. He said he had too much black ribbon so that he had to stuff it into the crown with dozens of pins."[2]

The drawings and paintings of "The White Plumes" are a return to naturalism for Matisse, but not at the expense of decorative abstract pattern. The rhythm of the looping ribbon, reiterated in the plumes and even Antoinette's hair, is his real subject.

P.F.B.

NOTES

[1]Alfred Barr, Jr., *Matisse: His Art and His Public*, New York, 1951, p. 206.

[2]Ibid.

PROVENANCE

Pierre Matisse Gallery, New York, 1932.

EXHIBITIONS

Cambridge, Fogg Art Museum, 1934; New York, Museum of Modern Art, 1944, p. 94 (repr.), Philadelphia Museum of Art, 1947, no. 170; Philadelphia Museum of Art, 1948, no. 117; Philadelphia Museum of Art, 1949; Cambridge, Fogg Art Museum, 1958; San Francisco, The California Palace of the Legion of Honor, 1962; Allentown Art Museum, 1977; Pittsburgh, Carnegie Institute, 1979; New York, Paul Rosenberg & Co., 1979.

LITERATURE

H. Matisse, *Cinquante dessins*, Paris, 1920, pl. XV; *Creative Art*, II, Nov., 1932, p. 210 (repr.); *Architect and Engineer*, 158, Aug., 1944, p. 4 (repr.).

Henri Matisse (1869-1954)

39. *Still-Life on Table (L'Ananas)*, 1925

Oil on canvas, 31¾ x 39¼ inches

Signed at bottom left: *Henri Matisse*

Lent by the Philadelphia Museum of Art, gift of Henry P. McIlhenny, retaining life interest.

This painting falls in Matisse's oeuvre after the bold fauvist pictures and their subsequent monumental development. While the avant garde of the dadaists, surrealists, and abstractionists of the 1920s raged about him, Matisse settled into a period of détente, solidifying the gains of the previous decades necessary for his subsequent growth.[1]

Elements of his favorite themes appear here: lemons and their shiny leaves, plums, anemones, backed by a decorative screen that partially blocks the depth of the painting. A plump pink pineapple rests in its bed of tissue, enhanced by the radiating halo of the lid of the basket. With the exception of this tissue (which is painted with a lush impasto), the paint is thinly applied. The apparent ease with which this ravishing picture was created belies the great intelligence of its organization of space. The work reflects a renewed meditation on these problems—set by Cézanne—which concerned Matisse in his early still-life paintings of 1909-11.

P.F.B.

NOTES

[1]See John Jacobus, *Henri Matisse*, n.d. [1972], p. 156.

PROVENANCE

Pacquement, Paris; Valentine Dudensing, Paris.

EXHIBITIONS

Basel, Kunsthalle, 1931; San Francisco Museum of Art, 1936; Philadelphia Museum of Art, 1937; New York, Museum of Modern Art, 1938; Boston, Museum of Modern Art, no. 35; Philadelphia Museum of Art, 1947, no. 76; Philadelphia Museum of Art, 1948, no. 64 (repr.); Philadelphia Museum of Art, 1949; San Francisco, The California Palace of the Legion of Honor, 1962; Allentown Art Museum, 1977; Pittsburgh, Carnegie Institute, 1979.

LITERATURE

Art News, 31, Nov. 19, 1932, p. 5 (repr.); A. Barr, *Matisse: His Art and His Public*, New York, 1951, p. 212.

Georges Rouault (1871-1958)
40. *Crucifixion*, ca. 1918

Oil and gouache on paper, 41¼ x 29⅝ inches

Signed at bottom right: *G. Rouault*

Lent by the Philadelphia Museum of Art, gift of Henry P. McIlhenny, retaining life interest.

German Expressionist painters such as Emil Nolde and Karl Schmidt-Rottluff were similarly motivated, but Rouault was unique among modern French artists in the religious conviction of his art.

Apprenticed to a maker of stained glass windows at age fourteen, Rouault's style evolved to incorporate the intensity of light filtering through colored glass, even simulating the lines of the lead dividers found in medieval church windows. This style rejected three-dimensional modeling in favor of large flat areas of color divided by thick black lines, or of similar color areas set into a black matrix.

Lionello Venturi finds in this picture the synthesis of the first part of Rouault's career: "At one stroke, one discovers the meaning and the justification of his new method. He remade himself primitive and of his time in order to arrive at God more boldly . . . Rouault had gone back through the course of the centuries until the moment where all images on earth function for God."[1] He had done this outside all established traditions, but with the fundamental beliefs of the artists of the fifteenth century. The impact of the *Crucifixion* is majestic, in the same way that an altarpiece by Masaccio is majestic: tempered by the sincerity of the artist's devotion.

P.F.B.

NOTES

[1]L. Venturi, *Georges Rouault*, New York, 1940, p. 52.

PROVENANCE

Pierre Matisse, New York, 1940.

EXHIBITIONS

Boston, The Institute of Modern Art (etc.), 1940, no. 8 (repr.); New York, Museum of Modern Art, 1944, repr. p. 45, p. 233; New York, Museum of Modern Art, 1945, no. 50, p. 71 (repr.); Philadelphia Museum of Art, 1947, no. 69; Philadelphia Museum of Art, 1949; New York, Museum of Modern Art, 1953, cat. p. 29; Boston Museum of Fine Arts, 1957, no. 123; San Francisco, The California Palace of the Legion of Honor, 1962; Allentown Art Museum, 1977; Pittsburgh, Carnegie Institute, 1979.

LITERATURE

Parnassus, II, Oct., 1939, p. 10 (repr.); C. Terrassé, *French Painting in the XXth Century*, Paris, 1939, p. 91 (repr.); L. Venturi, *Georges Rouault*, New York, 1940, p. 52, pl. 62; L. Venturi, *Georges Rouault*, Paris, 1948, pl. 53; *Studio*, 143, Apr., 1952, p. 105 (repr.); J. Maritain, *Rouault*, New York, 1952, p. 13 (repr. in color); P. Courthion, *Georges Rouault*, New York, 1961, pp. 420 and 462, no. 148 (repr.); S. Endo, etc., *Les Grands Maitres de la Peinture Moderne, Rouault et le Fauvisme*, Tokyo, 1973, p. 116, pl. 26 (repr. in color).

Georges Rouault (1871-1958)

41. *Sudarium of St. Veronica*, 1937

Oil on canvas, 11¾ x 9½ inches

Signed at bottom right: *G. Rouault*

The mystical legend of St. Veronica's Veil was one of the most fecund sources of imagery in medieval iconography. It is said that the Saint, on her way to market to sell her cloth, happened upon Christ in the procession to Calvary. She offered her veil to wipe away his blood and sweat, whereupon it became miraculously imprinted with the image of the suffering Christ's face. The legend found popularity in late medieval Netherlandish and German art, and eventually spread to Italy. The veil is sometimes shown in the larger context of the narrative of Calvary; but in those depictions which offer the veil alone, it seems magical—Christ's face superimposed as if a hallucination.

It is to this starkly simple manifestation of the icon that Rouault here returns. Stripped of its legend, it is a pathetic representation of suffering humanity, universal in its appeal. The icon appears at various times in his oeuvre, but is especially meaningful here on the eve of World War II.

P.F.B.

PROVENANCE

Pierre Matisse, New York.

EXHIBITIONS

Philadelphia Museum of Art, 1947, no. 95; Philadelphia Museum of Art, 1949; San Francisco, The California Palace of the Legion of Honor, 1962; Allentown Art Museum, 1977; Pittsburgh, Carnegie Institute, 1979.

John Constable (1776-1837)

42. *Coast Scene at Brighton*, ca. 1824-28

Oil on panel, 9 x 15⅛ inches

Constable's small sketches are unprecedented records of the conditions of atmosphere. The seascapes among them are considered to be the most "impressionist" of his works and were a decided influence on French landscape painting. While the direct impact of the English painter on the Impressionists is equivocal, his work stands as a testament to the general philosophical trend in the early nineteenth century which recognized naturalistic landscape as a legitimate subject of art. In this regard, his work is closest in spirit to that of the Barbizon School.

The small panel is enlivened with touches of white, creating a thoroughly convincing "impression" of the sea. It is this freedom of paint handling that inspired Delacroix (after making repeated trips to the Salon of 1824 to see the Constables) to repaint his *Massacre of Scio*.

P.F.B.

PROVENANCE

Captain Charles Golding Constable (sale 1890); John D. McIlhenny.

EXHIBITIONS

San Francisco, The California Palace of the Legion of Honor, 1962; Allentown Art Museum, 1977; New York, Metropolitan Museum of Art, 1983, no. 48.

Sir Edwin Landseer (1802-1873)

43. *The Bride of Lammermoor*, ca. 1830

Oil on panel, 13½ x 9 inches

Landseer met Sir Walter Scott on his first trip to the Highlands in 1824. They immediately struck up a strong friendship which would last until the author's death. They were in many ways kindred spirits, sharing at once great abilities for romantic narrative and also a love of the specific, telling detail.

Illustrations of Scott's novels supported many an artist; Landseer is known to have tried his hand at at least three, although only one—the subject here—was ever actually used in a book. This small and vivid painting was done in preparation for the engraved frontispiece to the 1830 Waverly edition of one of Scott's most popular novels, *The Bride of Lammermoor* (first published in 1818). Set in Scotland in the late 17th century, the novel tells the tragic love story of the Master of Ravenswood, heir to a ruined family, and Lucy Ashton, the daughter of the man who dispossessed him of his lands. While walking on the grounds of the castle, Lucy and her father are attacked by a wild bull, enraged by her red scarf. The bull charges, a shot rings out, Lucy faints as the bull collapses at her feet. The unknown savior who falls deeply in love with Lucy is, of course, the abused archenemy of her family, Ravenswood.

J.J.R.

EXHIBITIONS

Philadelphia Museum of Art and London, Tate Gallery, 1982, no. 69.

LITERATURE

A. Graves, comp., *Catalogue of the Works of the Late Sir Edwin Landseer*, Royal Academy of Arts, London, 1876, no. 155; C. Gordon, "The Illustration of Sir Walter Scott," *The Journal of the Warburg and Courtauld Institute*, vol. 34, 1971, pp. 309-310; R. Ormond, *Sir Edwin Landseer*, Philadelphia, 1982, pp. 115-116.

Sir Edwin Landseer (1802-1873)

44. *Ptarmigan*, ca. 1833

Oil on panel, 19¾ x 26 inches

The ptarmigan was the major sporting bird of the Highlands in Scotland, hiding in high rock shelves and requiring considerable stealth on the part of the hunter and his dogs to flush and bring down. Here, charged with as much emotion as he will bring to battling stags, Landseer demonstrates his remarkable ability to depict narrative animal subjects with the dimension of human tragedy. The male bird, his plumage treated with the delicacy and care of a still life, lies expiring on a rock. His mate, herself wounded, continues to guard the nest. As Richard Ormond has observed: "The bird on the left, head twisted in mute appeal and one leg stiffly extended, takes on the sublime nobility of a wounded hero while his mate . . . [has] the heroic echo of the theme of the widow, Hector and Andromache, and the world of human emotion. The other ptarmigan, sweeping across the great space behind (and the landscape is pitched in a high, romantic key) to the scene of the disaster, appear like a Greek chorus as harbingers of tragedy."

J.J.R.

PROVENANCE

William Wells, Redleaf (Sale: Christie's, May 10, 1890, lot 34); Agnew's, London; Mrs. Robert Frank, London.

EXHIBITIONS

London, British Institute, 1833, no. 129; London, Royal Academy of Arts, 1874, no. 352; London, Grovenor Gallery, 1890, no. 164; London, Royal Academy of Arts, 1961, no. 162; Detroit and Philadelphia, 1968, no. 173; Philadelphia and London, 1981, no. 37.

Sir Edwin Landseer (1802-1873)

45. *The Falconer: Mr. William Russell* (?), 1830s

Oil on canvas, 54½ x 43½ inches

Although this portrait has sometimes been thought to show Lord William Russell, son of the 6th Duke of Bedford, the age of the sitter makes it more likely that it is his son, also called William (1800-1884), one of Landseer's closest and most loyal friends. This is supported by a listing, among unfinished works, of a portrait of William Russell in Landseer's death sale in 1874, lot 304.

The 6th Duke of Bedford and his family, including his second wife, Giorgina, who was a great intimate of the artist and in all likelihood his mistress, were Landseer's first major patrons. Various children and grandchildren were portrayed, most happily as riding or hunting, Landseer always being shy of direct portraiture without some narrative element. Young William is shown with his falcon (falconry was undergoing a great revival in England in the 1830s), with a loyal hound pressed against his thigh. The immediate reference to 16th century Italian portraiture—particularly Titian's portraits of Charles V—is direct and certainly done to please.

Landseer was notorious for his frequent inability to finish works—particularly those involving friends—and the unfinished state of the picture probably explains the absence of an early exhibition record. This is for us one of the virtues of the picture—particularly when seen in the full gathering of Landseers in the McIlhenny collection. His speed of execution—just blocking in the forms with the wet brush—gives a great vitality to the picture and allows the one finished element, the face, to come through all the more effectively.

J.J.R.

PROVENANCE

Robert Wharton; Great Eastern Hotel, Liverpool Street Station, London (where it is reported to have hung on the staircase for many years); Agnew's, London (1959).

EXHIBITIONS

London, Royal Academy of Arts, 1961, no. 88; London, Arts Council (Hayward Gallery), 1974, no. 190.

Sir Edwin Landseer (1802-1873)

46. *Scotch Game*

Oil on panel, 18 x 23¾ inches

Landseer, despite his English orientation and training, was acutely aware of the grand traditions of earlier European painting. His pictures frequently use as their point of departure Dutch and Flemish works, many of which he would have known from the collections of his ducal friends and patrons.

Here, he has taken the 17th century Flemish notion of a dead game piece and made it his own. The day's trophies from hunting on the Scottish moors are arranged to depict the greatest nuances of colors and textures. Despite the formality of the subject, however, there is a troubled and horrific undertone, as if to suggest that, as beautiful as these elements are in the abstract, they are still the product of slaughter.

J.J.R.

PROVENANCE

T. H. Miller, probably Poulton le Fylde; Winston Guest; Wildenstein Gallery, New York.

EXHIBITIONS

London, Royal Academy of Arts, 1889.

Sir Edwin Landseer (1802-1873)

47. *Deer in Coldbath Fields, Woburn Park*

48. *Sheep, Woburn Park*

Oil on canvas, each 15¼ x 34 inches

These two charming pictures are reductions, with variations, of larger views of the park at Woburn, one of which (*Deer in Coldbath Fields*) continues to be in the family's collection with the Marquis of Tavistock. Given their scale and richly ornamented frames, they were probably initially intended for a specific architectural space, perhaps as overdoors.

The 6th Duke of Bedford's primary seat was the vast estate at Woburn Abbey. He and his family were extremely close to Landseer, providing him with some of his major early commissions (see no. 45). The family interests were broad and far ranging, the Duke particularly interested in agricultural and breeding reforms. He made his farms and livestock at Woburn a model of progressive attitudes and was especially proud of his deer herd (which included several exotic breeds), the descendants of which still lend picturesque romance to the great sweep of grounds surrounding the Abbey. These two pictures document the Duke's interest and evoke the sense of harmonious nature—the tame mixed with the wild—which is so critical to 18th and 19th century English sensibility.

J.J.R.

PROVENANCE

His Grace the Duke of Bedford; Leggett Gallery, London, 1951.

EXHIBITION

Christie's, London: Bedford Sale, January 19, 1951, lots 187 and 188.

LITERATURE

R. Ormond, *Sir Edwin Landseer*, Philadelphia, 1982, p. 167.

Sir Edwin Landseer (1802-1873)

49. *Night*, before 1853

50. *Morning*, before 1853

Oil on canvas, each 22½ x 35½ inches

Some of Landseer's most moving and effective subjects depict the terrible splendor of nature played out quite apart from man as witness or interferer. More than any other English artist of the 19th century, Landseer understood the grand theater of this Tennysonian world, in which magnificent beasts—especially the stags of the Scottish highlands—battled and ruled and, often, led themselves to their own destruction. Here, two contenders battle for the herd in a barren, moonlit landscape, the tumultuous lake echoing their mighty struggle; in the calm morning, both are dead, with the scavenger eagle and fox moving in with the dawn. This type of sentiment has, in our century, found better expression in film. However, the grandeur of the tragic epic here still holds its force.

J.J.R.

PROVENANCE
Viscount Hardings; Agnew's, London, 1956.

EXHIBITIONS
London, Royal Academy of Arts, 1853, nos. 46 and 69; The International Exhibition [n.d.], nos. 405 and 506; London, Royal Academy of Arts, 1874, nos. 295 and 506; London, Grovenor Gallery, 1890 (*Morning* only), no. 186; London, Christie's, sale June 1, 1956, lot 152.

LITERATURE
R. Ormond, *Sir Edwin Landseer*, Philadelphia, 1982, pp. 178-179.

Richard Ansdell (1815-1885)

51. *Lady and Gentleman on Horseback with a Keeper and Dead Stag*, 1847

Oil on canvas, 41 x 72 inches

Signed and dated at lower right: *Richard Ansdell; 1847*

Ansdell was born in Liverpool and, despite his permanent move to London in 1847, his most sustained reputation depended on his Merseyside patrons. His sporting subjects brought him considerable success, and while they rarely have either the vigor of treatment or visionary romanticism of his better known contemporary, Sir Edwin Landseer, there is a quality of gentle narrative and an ability to handle the illusive, pale light of the Highlands which supports the reputation he is now beginning to reclaim.

Here, in a picture thoroughly English in its attitudes and traditions, a young couple (tentatively identified as Mr. and Mrs. Naylor on their wedding trip in Scotland) are portrayed—*à la* "conservation group" with a local gilly who presents the garrotted stag just shot by the hero. It is not an uncommon scene; Landseer took it as a Royal Commission three years later, with his *Royal Sport on Hill and Loch* depicting the young Prince Albert presenting Queen Victoria with the trophies of his hunt. Yet, as Ansdell presents it, there is a singularly ungrand, understated tone to the narrative: the exhausted dogs, the slightly startled horse, the firm nobility of the gilly, and (to our modern perplexity) the calm demeanor of both the man and his bride. This down-to-earth pleasure in sport and almost thoughtless integration of man and nature is one of the most winning features of English painting of this kind, an attitude which continues the tradition of George Stubbs.

J.J.R.

PROVENANCE
Robert Frank, London, 1949.

James Collinson (ca. 1825-1887)
52. *For Sale*
53. *To Let*

Oil on canvas, each 23 x 18 inches

Collinson's fame today depends almost entirely on the two images exhibited here and the fact that he was one of the seven founding members (in 1848) of the Pre-Raphaelite Brotherhood, which was to so radically affect the history of English painting. His attachment to the Brotherhood, however, was tepid and short-lived; he only did one picture, the *Renunciation of Elizabeth of Hungary* (Municipal Art Gallery, Johannesburg), which reflects the fundamental tenets of the group, and he was probably drawn to them through his engagement to Christina Rossetti, the sister of Dante Gabriel and William. In 1850, he resigned from the Brotherhood and broke off his engagement, both acts prompted by his conversion to Roman Catholicism. After a period spent with the Jesuits at Stonyhurst, where he seems never to have found his vocation, he reemerged with a picture at the Royal Academy in 1855 and exhibited there some seventeen times until 1870. Following these religious and emotional crises, he seems to have rejected nearly all the principles of the Pre-Raphaelites. He was often the butt of jokes about his sleepy and unprepossessing manner, and he seems to have been content to produce interior genre of anecdotal and contemporary subjects.

The two subjects shown here were far and away his greatest successes, to judge from the number of replicas which exist, a unique occurrence in Collinson's work as far as we know. Pictures of this description were shown (although hung too high to receive anything but passing notice) at the Royal Academy in 1857. A version of *For Sale* entered the Castle Museum, Nottingham, in 1959 and is probably the mate to the *To Let* now in the Forbes Collection. Two others (with slight variations in details) now entitled *At the Bazaar* and *The Landlady* are in the Graves Art Gallery, Sheffield. They are the only signed and dated (1857 and 1856, respectively) versions and are perhaps the set exhibited at the Royal Academy. In 1919, another version of *For Sale*, called *The Empty Purse* (although without a pendant), was given to the Tate Gallery.

The placement of the McIlhenny pair within all these is unclear. Qualitatively, they hold their own perfectly well with the others; Collinson was noted, even while still with the Brotherhood, for his conscientious and steady working methods, so one would not expect too much variation in the handling of replicas. On the reverse of the McIlhenny *For Sale*, there is an old note which may eventually help unravel the puzzle. Faded and difficult to read, it calls them "*To Sell and To Let*" and continues, "*Newtown Park L30 . . .* [undecipherable] *on advance from Mr. Bishopson, the recruiting officer.*"

Given the charm of the figures and the bright loveliness of the color, their fame is not surprising. The subjects themselves, with the possible ambiguity of reading, may have contributed to their popularity (note the later renaming of some versions with less suggestive titles). It might be tempting to read into these works a commentary on the condition of women and their vulnerability to financial circumstances (the woman in *To Let* does wear a wedding ring)—in the spirit of such pictures as Collinson's contemporary Holman Hunt's moralizing *Awakening Conscience*—but this would give a false weight to this anecdotal artist.

J.J.R.

PROVENANCE

52: Mr. Bishopson, Newton Park (?); Montague Bernard, London.
53: Mr. Bishopson, Newton Park (?).

EXHIBITIONS

London, Royal Academy of Arts, 1857, no. 115 (?) and no. 102 (?).

LITERATURE

T. Bodkin, "James Collinson," *Apollo*, May 1940, pp. 128-133; C. Forbes, *The Royal Academy Revisited: Victorian Paintings from the Forbes Magazine Collection*, Princeton University, Art Museum, 1975, pp. 30-31; *Great Victorian Pictures*, London, Royal Academy of Arts (Arts Council), 1978, p. 28.

BAZAAR

Sir Edward Lear (1812-1888)

54. *Zurich See: Switzerland*, 1854

Pen, brown ink and pencil, 12¾ x 19¾ inches

Inscribed with color notes and dated: *September 26th, 1854*

Edward Lear is best known for his enchanting nonsense verse, a genre in which he is still the unexcelled master. Yet he was one of the most prolific topographical landscape draftsmen of his day. He was wildly peripatetic—almost compulsively so—and was a figure of remarkable spirit and energy. Yet despite the warm patronage which he received early in his life and the vast array of friends who received his wonderfully humorous letters and drawings, his life was in many ways poignant. He was troubled by ill health and felt a need to distance himself from his friends through his extensive travels.

Often his landscape views on paper are worked up in color and touches of white, probably for his own amusement after his return to the studio but also to "finish" them for readier sale. This brilliantly fresh drawing has escaped these efforts and has a remarkably vivid sense of both the place itself—the fields sloping down to the lake with the grand mountains in the distance—and also of the artist's own pleasure in setting it down properly.

J.J.R.

PROVENANCE
Noortman and Brod, New York, 1983.

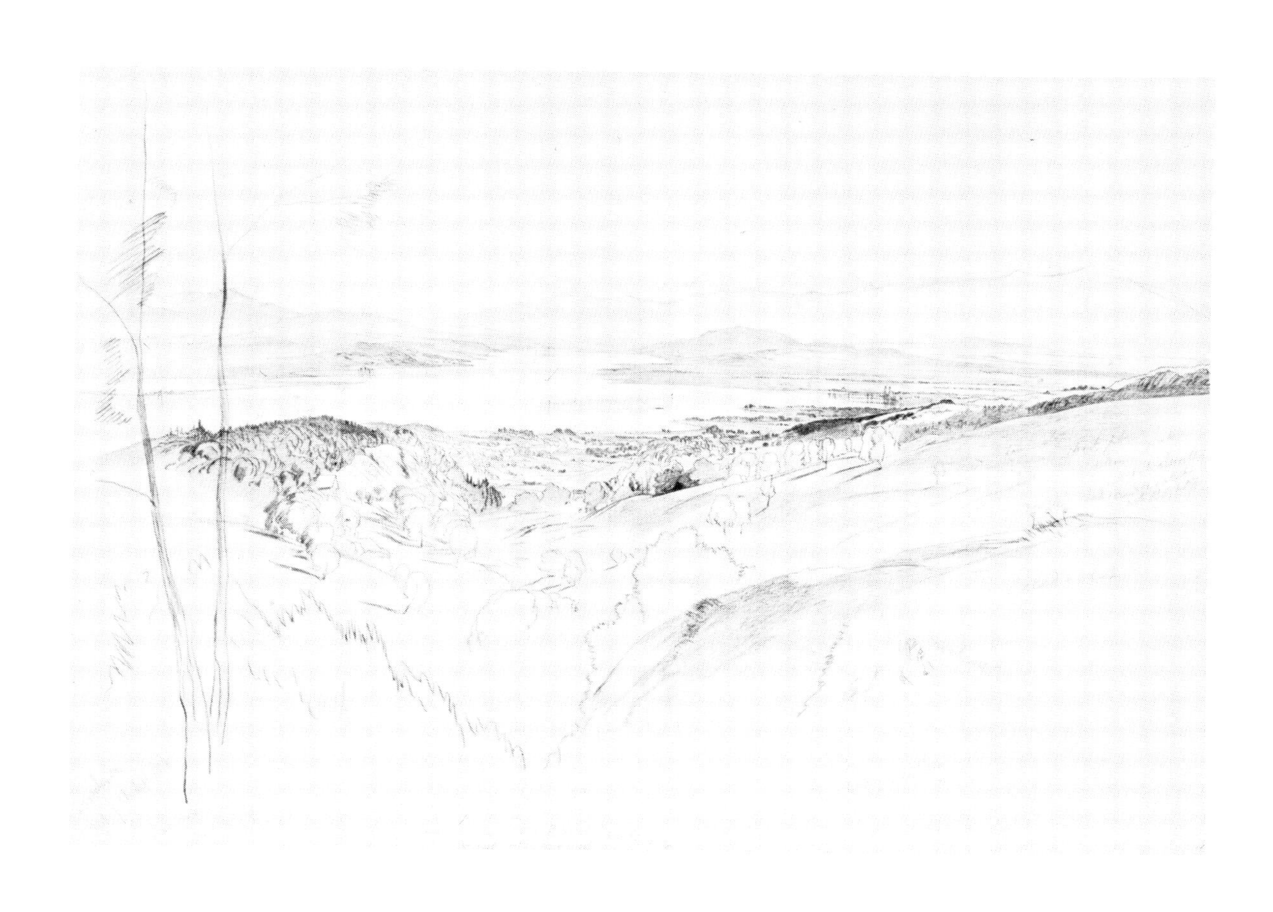

Sir Edward Lear (1812-1888)

55. *Mahabalipuram*, 1881

Oil on panel, 9½ x 18¼ inches

Inscribed in script at lower left: *Mahabeleheorem*

Signed (with a monogram) and dated at lower right: *1881*

Despite his rather advanced age (and the uncertain health which plagued him throughout his life), Lear set out for India in November 1873 on the invitation of the newly appointed Viceroy, Lord Northbrook. He toured the entire subcontinent as well as Ceylon (Sri Lanka) until January 1875. This was the last important voyage of his life and one which would, from his drawings and watercolors done on the spot, provide considerable resources for his painting in oil after he returned to his home in the South of France.

As was typical of Lear, particularly in the oil paintings done some time after his actual visit to a site, he attempts to give a general sense of the place rather than to give specific topographical information. Mahabalipuram, on the Bay of Bengal in the southeast province of Madras, is one of the most important (and best preserved) temple sites of early Hinduism. However, Lear only depicts two weathered structures—isolated shrines to Durga and Shiva to judge from contemporary photographs of the site—and is content to evoke the lush isolation of the place. It is a picture painted with great energy—the palm fronds take on a schematic, flame-like pattern—more reflective of Lear's memory of the place than his precise observations.

J.J.R.

PROVENANCE

Alfred Symour; Agnew's, London.

Index of Artists

The Henry P. McIlhenny Collection:
Nineteenth Century French and English Masterpieces
High Museum of Art, Atlanta

ISBN 0-939802-21-X